SECOND THOUGHTS

SECOND THOUGHTS

REFLECTIONS ON LITERATURE AND ON LIFE

❧ BY FRANÇOIS MAURIAC

THE WORLD PUBLISHING COMPANY

❧ CLEVELAND AND NEW YORK

PUBLISHED BY The World Publishing Company

2231 WEST 110TH STREET, CLEVELAND 2, OHIO

PUBLISHED SIMULTANEOUSLY IN CANADA BY

NELSON, FOSTER & SCOTT LTD.

Library of Congress Catalog Card Number: 61-5803

First Edition

Translated by Adrienne Foulke

CONTENTS

PART ONE: LITERATURE

1. On Writing Today

2. And on Writers

Contents

PART TWO: LIFE

1. The First Day of the Year

2. The Ages of Man—and Woman

3. On War

Contents

4. On Nature

PART ONE: LITERATURE

1. On Writing Today

THE DETACHMENT OF THE ARTIST

During the summer of '39, when Paris was in a tumult of public tension, a Cézanne exhibit at the Orangerie acquired, by force of contrast, a special significance. I was troubled and divided in mind whenever I went to see it, but each time I came away with a renewed conviction that the artist's vocation springs fundamentally from his selflessness. And Cézanne reminded me that the more people surrender to violent partisanship the more they need the disinterested detachment of a few men.

It is a wonderful thing that Montaigne should have meditated on man and the human condition in the midst of the darkest of religious wars. The bloody horror of that conflict fortified him in his mission as observer and witness. He was the one attentive reporter in a country gone mad: "Others mold man," he wrote, "but I set him forth." He never claimed for a moment to do more than to describe us or to set us forth, yet it is he who actually molds us by offering us an exact image of ourselves. Thanks to him, we can slip through the net cast by progressive Plans and benevolent Systems to ensnare us. And man as he truly is—man as Montaigne and Pascal saw him, the creature of flesh and spirit—must always be able to escape those fearsome fishermen.

It is Montaigne's business and not ours that he wrote the *Essais* only for his own pleasure and had no particular desire to help his fellow man. During the '30s it was fashionable to berate Paul Valéry because he pretended to care about nothing but the technique of his art, about the poetic means he used and his own awareness of them. In the same way, some people scoffed at Proust because he was unable to do more than "watch himself feel or think or speak." His monstrous curiosity, which was neither selective nor critical in the strict sense, was accounted a near crime. But why does it matter to us what the impulse may be that makes a man write as he does? Suppose that *Jeune Parque* did result from the experiments of a man absorbed by problems of prosody, and the *A la recherche du temps perdu* from the use a sickly man made of his cloistered solitude? We are nonetheless indebted to them for a portion of our greatest wealth—wealth that has nothing to do with gold bullion meticulously weighed and stored in a vault but that is actively, nourishingly, endlessly creative.

Our young people today insist that we must "think with our hands," that is, with a view to acting directly on our fellowmen. They profess that intellectual labor must be directed toward a concrete end. According to them, the gratuitous has had its day, and the people expect their mentors to supply only useful facts and directives. I wonder if they really believe that Montaigne and his kind did not influence human affairs? I wonder if the gratuitousness of a work is not often the measure both of its potency in depth for human beings as well as of its ability to endure in time?

The truth of the matter is that the action of a Montaigne is not like a bombshell's. It is easy to follow a man's trail in the political and social realm. The furrow turned up by Karl Marx, for example, is visible to the naked eye. But the saunterings of Montaigne or Pascal or Proust, the obscure modifications wrought on the élite of mankind by Mozart or Cézanne, are of another order and escape our grasp. What was conceived in a spirit of contempt for the immediate by men who stood apart from their times and were indifferent to its preoccupations, classifications, plans, and systems—this is what proves with time to be quite literally overwhelming. How many of the great, eternally alive and potent books were born of some personal, unknown drama and had no connection with contemporary concerns!

There are, as we all realize, some of the other kind. We know the type of creative person that some of our young people are demanding but cannot find among their elders or, struggle as they visibly do, can they call forth, deliver, indeed forcibly rip from themselves. A lyrical philosopher like Nietzsche comes to mind: a man who would not think the search an end in itself, and who would be convinced that he held a monopoly on the formula to insure human happiness. Or perhaps a poet, the heir of a Péguy, whose inspiration springs from the earth and, far from being soiled thereby, is nourished and enriched by all the passions of the moment.

I have always thought that this philosopher-poet was born some forty or fifty years ago, and that he is resting today somewhere between the sea and the Vosges or in the shadow of a wooden cross at Salonica, or in the Dardenelles, or down, down on the ocean floor—unless God, who knows what he might have become, has granted him the burial under the Arc de Triomphe that he would have been awarded after a long life filled with glory had he not been killed at the age of twenty.

A CRITIQUE OF CRITICISM

If one is to believe them, the majority of my fellow writers do not bother to read what is published about their books. In my own case, neither time nor habit has been able to dull the pleasure it gives me to run through press clippings every morning. I don't think that I tally up my score out of any particular professional vanity. More than once I have not even finished some fervid eulogy, whereas I will reread a panning two or three times if it throws any light on my book or on myself or on the personality of the critic.

What hope could there be for a writer who is nearing the end of his life but who is still unable to judge his own judges impartially or to benefit from the flood of contradictory opinions that assails him every morning?

I make an effort to read each critic with an open mind, except for the very few whose judgment is corrupted by concerns alien to literature. (From long experience we know that the book section in this or that paper gives the exact temperature reading of our relations with whatever political party the paper represents.)

If you read heavy doses of criticism—and that is the only way it is administered these days—you encounter many conflicting opinions, but one very definite impression emerges none the less. With a few notable exceptions, critics condemn and reject what is most particularly and intimately the writer's own.

In this connection, I might say, I find it significant that the critics should be nearly unanimous in reproaching one author I know quite well for his choice of characters. The hero of *Les anges noirs,* Gabriel Gradère, is blood brother to a Carco gangster. As Carco would envisage him, Gradère would be anything but frightening; actually, he would seem almost normal, because his situation would not raise any question of eternity. Carco possesses the unique gift of making dope-trafficker, pimp, or blackmailer seem familiar and close to us.

I do the opposite. In spite of myself, I invest a metaphysical dimension in all my characters, and this makes for uneasiness in the reader. I am a metaphysician who works in the concrete. I exploit a certain gift for creating atmosphere to make the Catholic universe of evil palpable, tangible, pungent. The theologians offer us an abstract idea of the sinner; I present him in flesh and blood.

So when the critic complains about my characters, his criticism misfires because my people are everyday people. He should really not belabor them but me and whatever it is that makes every creature I put my hand to develop instantly into that dreadful and indefensible thing called "a Mauriac character."

Similarly, when the critic decides that you are not a real novelist and your novel is not a true novel, when he undertakes to demolish you totally by comparing you with Balzac or Dostoevski, he is rejecting precisely that which differentiates you from these great forebears —your self.

To tell an author who claims he has written a classical tragedy: "Your play is not a classical tragedy, because it has fewer than five acts and does not observe the three laws of unity" is legitimate but it is absurd to base the canon of the novel on Balzac or Tolstoy or Flaubert, and to exclude from the category of "novel" any book that departs from the type that criticism considers —on its own authority—the one and only true novel.

It is precisely differences and deviations that give the novelist his chance to survive. No one should construe this as vanity. Every literary period, I believe, jettisons the bulk of its fictional cargo and, accordingly, our individual chances of surviving are minimal. But if we writers had the good luck to reach a remote shore of the future, it would be thanks to everything in our work that is irreducibly our own, even to the very faults that limit us and prevent our measuring up to our predecessors.

Today no one thinks of reproaching Manet for having painted Manets. But while Manet was alive, he was reproached for being Manet. "When will Monsieur X paint happy lovers and normal, decent people? When will he write novels as long as Dostoevski's? When will he concern himself with social problems? When will he be less facile? When will he follow a bent other than his own?"

An author can be more or less affected when such charges and demands are leveled at him. (Especially if a critic says severely to his face, as happened to me the other day: "Your book tells me things about you that I had never suspected." Now I don't have a strangler's hands, but instinctively I thrust my hands deep in my pockets!) Yes, under the influence of my critics, I have often dreamed of writing the story of a saintly little girl, a sister of Thérèse Martin. I have fancied that Mozart, who opened the gates of his paradise to me, might suddenly let loose in my books a flock of angels who would not be black. But the moment I set to work, everything becomes colored by my abiding concerns: my most beautiful characters move into a certain sulphurous light that is peculiar to me and that I do not defend—it is simply mine.

"M. Mauriac has signed the decree that condemns him to be M. Mauriac for life," one young upstart wrote recently about my latest book. Is this a death sentence? No, it is a life sentence—or, more exactly, a parole. What saves an author in literary terms—if he is to be saved—is his absolute inability to be anyone but himself. An artist who can be someone other than himself, who is all painters or all writers in turn, is lost before he starts. How could he last if he does not exist? Only to the extent to which the conscious will enters into my writing (out of scruple, a fear of shocking the reader, etc.) do I feel threatened.

In my opinion, a good critic who must judge an author will not insist that he be someone else; he will look to see if in the work under consideration the author was able to remain faithful to the laws of his own universe, if he employed only his own native gifts and did not resort to formulas or fashions. The critic should demand that the novelist not deny himself, that he not puff himself up in order to imitate anyone. In my view, it is reprehensible for the critic to indulge in invidious comparisons to demolish the work he is examining, for our problem as writers is not to follow in the footsteps of the great masters but to realize, each one of us to the full, the modest artist that he himself is. May each of us try to exhaust his own potential without trying to exceed it—that is what every good critic should demand of us. No universal law exists that allows him to damn us. A good critic looks for no touchstone beyond the author he is studying.

If a genuine writer produces a failure, it is never because he has broken this or that rule of the genre, for there are no recipes for the production of a good novel; he fails because he has been unfaithful to the secret code that allowed Colette to write *Chéri* for example, and Chardonne to write *Les destinées sentimentales.* The Code Colette is without value for Chardonne, and if Colette ever ventured into the atmosphere of Chardonne's environment, she would die of asphyxiation. Let us be judged—if necessary, let us be condemned—by our own law alone.

II

M. Robert Brasillach is willing to grant me one point at least: that a critic should not allow himself to swamp the book he is examining by crushing comparisons with the work of a Balzac or a Tolstoy. In his opinion, however, the critic cannot avoid such confrontations when he wants to adjudge the rank a contemporary author will hold in literary history, the task of the critic being, according to him, to anticipate the verdict of posterity.

I think such prophecies are useless and idle. One should see them for what they are, a scholastic habit; it is as if we thought we were still in the classroom. When I was a boy, I considered Lamartine and Hugo to be without peers; de Musset (Alfred) came second; de Vigny (Alfred) came third; de Laprade (Victor) and Delavigne (Casimir) fourth; etc. But which writers mattered to us most, which still help us to live? Where

are those companions of our youth who left a deeper
mark on us than any living friend? The authors whose
names come to mind first are unclassifiable.

What place, for example, should one assign Maurice
de Guérin, that child among the pontiffs of romanti-
cism? After Guérin's death, George Sand published an
essay on him in the *Revue des deux mondes,* to the
amazement of Lacordaire. Lacordaire had known
Maurice—*let's see, certainly, a distinguished young man
indeed*—but in the eyes of the great Dominican, that's
all he was, the most insignificant of the disciples
Lamennais had attracted to La Chesnaie. Two prose
poems, a private journal, a few youthful letters—truly
nothing there to dazzle one, among all the *glorious*
works created in his time. And yet how many of us
there are who love Maurice, who feel that he is still
very close to us, who hear him breathing in our room
when, for the hundredth time, we open his journal to
such and such a page.

Similarly, Sainte-Beuve was not wrong to set *Les
fleurs du mal* beyond the frontiers of normal literature
in the far reaches of a literary Siberia. It is impossible
to compare the volume of Baudelaire and the immense
mass of Victor Hugo without crushing the former.
Arthur Rimbaud could likewise not be entered on any
official honors list. Is it by chance that all the special
cases that come to mind are poets whose undis-
tinguished or non-existent status in the manuals of
literature has no relation to the place they occupy in

the hearts of those few Frenchmen who still care about poetry?

The real question for the critic is not to know if such and such an author is as important as Balzac or Tolstoy, but whether he exists as a "planet," whether in himself he constitutes a complete world of a kind that a few men can approach, a familiar world that they prefer above all others.

Posterity classifies the "stars" in order of their importance, but there is grandeur and grandeur: if Hugo is incomparably greater than Rimbaud, the power of Rimbaud over those who cherish him is of an altogether different potency from that of Hugo over his admirers. Whose inner life has ever been changed by Hugo? Whereas *Les illuminations* and *Une saison en enfer* gave Claudel as a young man an almost physical perception of the invisible world.

What is the point of trying to foresee the classification posterity will establish? It will not be definitive in any case; a hundred years after an author has died people can be still arguing about him. On the other hand, and to the extent that we are endowed with a critical sense, we ought to approach a literary work as if it were a continent; to study its flora and fauna, its climate and terrain; to determine if it is habitable, if a spiritual colony has a chance to survive there, living off the resources of the land and discovering new natural wealth.

This last point is essential. Very great works, like those of Hugo or Lamartine, render up promptly what they have to offer; their treasure has been sorted out and inventoried for all time. But other works that seem to be much more limited and confined allow themselves to be explored only slowly. There are rich layers that the prospector does not immediately detect; a good critic is the sorcerer who makes some hidden spring gush forth unexpectedly under our feet. And what does it matter to us that the supply of water be small or even intermittent, if it refreshes us more than the vast official Niagaras?

If I were permitted to speak freely about the work of my contemporaries, I would endeavor to establish this distinction between those who seem to me "possible living worlds" and the "dead stars," those which, for all their brilliance, will finally fade from sight. One would also have to set aside those books that may last, but only as museum pieces that we walk past without dreaming of casting them in the secret drama of our life.

For that matter, what does it mean to say that an author will endure? Is one speaking about the author or his books? They are not the same thing. The number of literary works that survive outside the anthologies and textbooks, that are and always will be read and meditated upon, like Montaigne's essays or Racine's tragedies, those that still influence individual destinies —such books are extremely rare.

Most often, it is the author himself who interests us, and we retain only the passages from his books that tell us about him; we scarcely read Rousseau today except for the *Confessions,* or Chateaubriand aside from *Memoires d'outre-tombe;* of Voltaire we read the *Correspondance*—and *Candide.*

These great men have survived their own works, and we too, small as we may be, tiny as our possibility of survival may be, have a better chance than do our books. If any pages manage to keep afloat, they will be those that throw some light on our unknown life.

"Exactly!" someone will object. When we compare a living author with his august elders, we do so to judge whether or not his work is the kind that exists independently of the author, if it possesses the classic characteristic of surviving on its own merit; *Andromaque* and *Phèdre* interest us far more than Racine does.

The critic runs no great risk if he is pessimistic on this score. Most books belong to a short-lived race; they are born and they die before our eyes, thus enabling writers to replace them promptly by a process of uninterrupted parturition in which, almost to a man, they demonstrate formidable fertility and appalling regularity.

THE CYCLICAL NOVEL

I don't know exactly what the public thinks of cyclical novels; I would guess that most readers do not dread length though they dislike prolixity. As for authors, I find it amazing that a novelist can decide in advance that he will not finish a work without one or more sequels and publicly announces as much. Actually, a real writer never has any hint of whether his book will be born as a river, stream, or brook. It took Balzac a long time to realize that he was writing *La comédie humaine.* As he himself said, when the idea did dawn on him, it seemed like a wild dream. "It was after the fact, after a strenuous and ingenious labor of organization," George Sand relates, "that he wrought out of all the parts of his work a coherent and profound whole. . . . This job of organization occupied him for the last years of his life. . . ."

Authors who are in ill repute because their books are "too short" can take comfort from this illustrious example. And what is to prevent them from devoting their old age to a search for the ties that bind all the sons and daughters their imaginations have spawned? Without any juggling, either, for an author is parent to many offspring.

I have no quarrel to pick with a long novel but only with an inflated one, a novel that is blown up for the sake of size alone. Nothing is more spurious, I think, than to consider length a warrant of superiority. *War and Peace* is a masterpiece; *The Death of Ivan Ilich* is another. Each obeyed its own law; for the former it was the law of abundance, and for the latter, of compression and condensation.

I also think it is a serious mistake for us writers to attach any importance to the number of characters we invent: to try to keep all our troops in the field, for example; or to drop one creature who is full of life

and runs on ahead, pulling us along with him, simply
because we think it is another's turn; quite possibly,
the second is only asking to be allowed to sleep a while
longer; he has a valid claim on a chapter of his own
but must wait for the right developments.

Another odd misconception holds that an author
comes closer to real life by multiplying the number of
his heroes. In the course of one hour more people pass
by on the left sidewalk from the Madeleine to the Café
de la Paix than you could sketch in the most torrential
of cyclical novels. A fifteen-volume novel may be as remote from reality as *La Princesse de Clèves* or *Adolphe*.

The Anglo-Saxons and the Russians have a gift for
creating these vast worlds of fiction into which we, being
French, love to follow them. We enjoy losing ourselves,
we are all the more responsive to their charm because
we know that we cannot imitate such writers. Theirs
is a profoundly outgoing instinct. They go out to meet
life, they can let themselves be carried away by it. Without worrying about external order or formal logic, they
are able to assimilate an inner law of life. But a willful,
logical French fellow, good son of Descartes that he is,
becomes all involved in constructing his fictional universe, and he goes about it by following a method that
is, he knows, infallible. This is an absorbing experiment to watch, even though one can never feel com-
pletely confident of the outcome. One of Descartes's
principles was "to divide each of the difficulties into as
many parts as is possible and as is required the better
to resolve them." In fiction this means that each char-

acter must cover the course at the appointed hour, the author-manager hardly reserving the right to make changes in the schedule.

The French writer who embarks on an outsize book never gives in to the current of life, he never lets himself be swept along by the tide. He remains fearfully lucid and mindful of every detail. He reminds himself of another rule Descartes set for himself: "To keep such complete accounts and to make such comprehensive reviews as to permit me to be confident that nothing has been omitted." With this in mind, our author pauses at the end of every fourth volume, tallies up his characters, measures the distance traveled, smiles amiably at the public—and is pleasantly astonished, I should think, to discover that it has stayed with him so long.

Such troubles are negligible, I hasten to say, if the novelist in question is also a great poet, as in the case of Jules Romain. In the early volumes of *Les hommes de bonne volonté,* we continually feel that poetic power is about to sweep away splendid regimentation and introduce some vital confusion into a world revised and set in order by an academic god. In the early phases of the long voyage on which M. Romain takes us, I am acutely aware of this moving struggle between the creator's organizing drive, his will to dominate, and the restiveness of his shackled characters.

My young colleagues must not place too much dependence on his august example. Another way of "writing long" is to be unselective, to fail to cut; the resulting quantity is no sign of true abundance nor does it certify any work for undying fame. The biggest books can perish as readily as the smallest. Throughout literature we have seen Titanics flounder and sink, all hands and cargo lost, while nutshells have floated down to us from the springs of time.

These observations clearly do not apply to the French cyclical novels that have achieved great and merited success. Nor are they intended to mitigate the harsh criticism commonly leveled at the short novel. Often the short novel has latent values that its author has failed to exploit. Its brevity is not always necessary, but simply the result of laziness in a writer whose talent, to reverse the famous definition, is an all too brief impatience. Since the war, certainly, we have sensed the complicity of publishers, critics, and public in fostering what I will call the short-order writer. The snack bars of literature take precedence over restaurants, as it were, dispensing real food.

So when new writers attempt long works we must give them their due for having surmounted all this impatience and haste, but at the same time must put them on their guard against the mammoth novel. They think they are giving themselves free rein; actually, these immense projects threaten to become their suffocating prisons.

To my way of thinking, what helps a writer persevere in his work and overcome his weariness and distaste for it is that, as he begins each new book, he feels as if he were facing an unknown world that has no apparent bond with the preceding one. He has the illusion—entirely salutary—that up to this point he has produced only rough drafts of the masterpiece he is about to create. And although he knows in his heart that it will fall short of his expectations, hope still whispers, "Who knows? . . . Maybe this time . . ." I, for one, would never be able to stand the misery of dragging the ball and chain of my earlier books about with me. What has been published has gone out from me, and for me it is dead. It is wonderful to set out on a fresh effort, full of apprehension and hope for what will emerge; wonderful not to know what I will be wanting to write in six months, in a year; wonderful to be always available, to let the imagination wander where it will. It shall not be swallowed up in one of those great empty edifices people try to force it into, I tell myself. Indeed, I am free to follow my fancy. I can desert the twenty-five volume workshop! But will I have the strength and courage, or indeed the interest, to come back to it later? I doubt it, for unfinished buildings do not make lovely ruins.

A FORGOTTEN BOOK

Nothing sensitizes us more keenly to the passing of time and the rupture in us between the aging adult and the quixotic youth, nor is there anything more disconcerting than to reread a book we passionately admired in our youth and to find it now, amazingly enough, so awfully feeble. I felt this again in the last few days while rereading Romain Rolland's *Antoinette,* which I came across in a cupboard here in my home in the country. I first read it when it was published as one volume in the *Jean-Christophe* cycle, and I remember weeping copiously over it.

I see, I think, what it is that changes: it is our enthusiasms. *We* remain the same, *we* do not change; we simply lose the power that we possess when we are young to invest the gloomiest object with our own light, to kindle it with a fire that comes from youth itself. We do not change, but we lose, little by little, the power to embellish and to transfigure.

I had given some thought to this once before, when I went to the retrospective exhibit of French painting at the Palais du Quai de Tokio. Only one canvas of Eugène Carrière was shown, and in that long, dazzling chain, that river of light that flows from the Master of Moulins to Manet to Cézanne, Carrière was a dull link indeed, a kind of gray puddle. Yet how I used to love him! I could stand and muse for hours before those canvases with their dense atmosphere of "everyday tragedy," as we used to put it, mindful of Maeterlinck; those faces, sculptured, one would have said, in their own mystery, with their confused drama only partially expressed, plunged us into long daydreams. Even today, Carrière's "maternity" paintings preserve their feeling of humanity; his Christ still moves me, and Mary, as she stands at the foot of the Cross suppressing a sob, always makes me think of a line of Jammes: *"Avec ce gonflement de douleur qui étouffe. . . ."* But his work has nothing do do with the history of painting; perhaps it is closer to sculpture, a kind of trompe-l'oeil sculpture, in which the clay would be viscous and smeared. Carrière's art has only a very remote connection with the art of men who assemble and arrange colors in a certain relation and order, and are therefore called painters.

Romain Rolland's adventure is of another kind. His *Jean-Christophe* occupies an important place in the literary history of emotional sensibilities in the early twentieth century, but *Antoinette,* which I used to single out as a superlative jewel, is like every other novel of the period. Its composition follows a tested recipe. Maybe it is not bad, maybe not even mediocre; let's say that it has the merit of showing us what the catch-penny success of 1910 was like.

The first thing to impress us when we reread a bestseller of that period is that as we have grown older each of us has formed a certain idea of style. It may be arbitrary or debatable, but in its terms we irrevocably judge works of the intellect. Often one paragraph, even one sentence is enough to disenchant us and make us turn our back on an author and escape from his dominion forever. If a stranger were to bring me the manuscript of *Antoinette* today, I would certainly break off at the chapter ending on page fifty-six: "When people feel threatened," Rolland writes, "they are prone to behave like the ostrich; they hide their heads and imagine that misfortune cannot see them."

Probably I would be wrong to stop reading at that point. It happens to the best of authors: a writer succumbs to a handy metaphor that has been lying around too long, picks up something no one else would dare touch. But the fact remains that such a trivial detail stops me dead in my tracks today whereas it would not have so much as ruffled my twentieth year.

We enjoy the impression—or illusion—of having acquired with maturity a sense of the authentic, which we had scarcely or, at least, to a much lesser degree possessed before, and this governs our judgments. I am not considering the whole of *Jean-Christophe* now but only *Antoinette,* which seemed to me such a rare and exceptional book years ago, and which I now see as second-rate. There is virtually nothing spontaneous in it, nothing that savors of an experience captured at the source.

I am mindful of how unjust it may seem to accuse this book of being unauthentic many years after its publication. It will be argued that if the portrait of the young girl that once seemed to me as real as life itself now appears to be falsely drawn, we must look beyond the book for the reasons, to an evolution of customs, a change of atmosphere, the passage of time.

Perhaps not. The passage of time has nothing to do with it. In the last chapter of *L'éducation sentimentale,* Flaubert's hero, Frédéric Moreau, says to Mme. Arnoux, "It excites me to see your foot. . . ." This may seem laughable to the reader who is accustomed to seeing his girl in shorts and to taking sun baths with her.

Still, he has positively no doubt about Frédéric's feeling when he saw Mme. Arnoux's foot. Time does not nibble away at anything in a novel which was true in the period when the book was written and which, in relation to that period, will always remain true. On the other hand, time points a cruel finger at the false detail or observation, and these are not lacking in *Antoinette.*

For example, Mme. Jeannin is married to a provincial banker who goes bankrupt and kills himself. She takes refuge in Paris, where her sister, now the wife of a wealthy and important official, is living. A writer knows nothing of the French middle class if he proceeds to relate that the rich relative (and she can be as predatory a woman as M. Romain Rolland wants) lends her widowed sister and young nephews two hundred francs and shows them the door. If she were to do such a thing, it would be an instance of unusual behavior which the author would have to make credible. Whether out of self-love or family pride or fear of what people would say, the sister will assure her relatives bread and board and the wherewithal to maintain their position and to keep face, but she will make them pay for it by a day-in-day-out martyrdom that is in itself a meaty subject.

Reliance on this kind of fake tragedy struck me particularly in *Antoinette.* I had preserved a harrowing recollection of the meeting of Antoinette and Jean-Christophe: their trains pass each other and stop for a moment in a station, so that they are able to exchange only a glance through the train windows. What I had forgotten, and what dismays me, I admit, is that the author is so taken with his device that he repeats it a few pages farther on and shows us Antoinette and Jean-Christophe in a Paris street separated forever by a throng of carriages and a felled horse! How could I have ever responded to such heavy-handed effects? I was able to because I identified myself with Olivier, Antoinette's brother. I was the hero of the book.

The young reader is better able to sustain illusion and transform what he reads because he enters into a book the way a stream enters into a river and mingles with it. His own life inflates the life of the fictional characters; he retains from what he reads only that which allows him to watch himself live in another person. Antoinette's dubious tragedy became true by being refracted through me.

This, in any case, was only one episode in the whole book. The story ends with the study of the friendship between Olivier and Jean-Christophe, which, as I remember, seemed to me the most moving development in the whole of this prewar cyclical novel. Novelists are forever studying love, but it is not so prevalent a passion in early youth as people pretend. We dream of love long before we experience it, whereas friendship, which is young people's daily bread and which occupies such an important place in their lives, is almost never dealt with in books. Antoinette died, and Olivier met Jean-Christophe. I think I remember feeling that at this point the story recaptured some authentic quality, but would I swear to it? Perhaps the better part of valor is not to look back, but rather to break off a dangerous experiment.

I am still convinced that *Jean-Christophe* is worthy of the admiration we once offered it. But it is better, I think, to stop on a note of affectionate recollection; the greatest kindness we can show some authors of our youth is not to reread them. I can imagine that, some day—far, far in the future—an elderly, seasoned critic (one of my younger friends of the moment) will reread these remarks on a forgotten novel, and show me the same charity that I extend to Romain Rolland: he will advise his readers not to disturb the eternal sleep of my books.

LITERATURE AND SIN

On December 21, 1939, a fearsome tirade was loosed from the pulpit of the Church of Saint Roch, in Paris. "God forbid," thundered the Bishop of Mans, "God forbid that I should seek to clip the wings of genius! But is it not true that, under the pretext of artistic freedom, certain writers and artists presume to reconcile the audacities of their pen and brush with the practice of the sacraments?" And Monsignor Grente proceeded to denounce with a vigor altogether apostolic "these men who congratulate themselves on their own piety the while they confuse and pervert their fellow men!"

Let me hasten to reassure those persons to whom I am indebted for their consuming zeal in bringing this sermon to my attention. To all these good souls I bring news that will rejoice their hearts. The Saint-Roch reprimand was not directed at my unworthy self. I have this on the best authority. In the course of several meetings which the Bishop of Mans was good enough to grant me in the old days when he did not disdain to glance in the direction of our writing fraternity, I had the consolation of learning from his own lips that he was not only charmed but even greatly edified by my books.

However, even if the arrow was not aimed at me, dare I deny that it struck me all the same? What Catholic writer, whether novelist or dramatist, has not often had to pluck it from his flesh? Without meaning to, the Bishop of Mans put his finger on an incurable wound. There is no help for it: sin is the writer's element; the passions of the heart are the bread and wine he savors daily. Maritain urges us to describe them but not to connive in them, and doubtless for the philosopher as well as the moralist this is within the realm of the possible. But it is not possible for the imaginative writer, whose whole art consists in making visible, tangible, and odorous a world as fraught with criminal delights as with saintliness. This is the rock we are anchored to, and we will cling to it until the day we die. May Grace none the less abide in our work; may the reader everywhere sense the subterranean flow, the communion of love, even when it is seemingly derided or denied.

Even so, our novels and plays would have horrified most of the saints we venerate. If believing contemporaries are more indulgent, I am afraid they are giving in to a personal sympathy. We realize that there are religious individuals, consecrated priests, lofty spirits, who have a weakness for us. This is not blind love (love is the most lucid of passions) but the slightly blurred friendliness from which writers benefit occasionally and which, I firmly believe, means enough to them spiritually to help them not lose heart. Even if such affection is not deserved, it will follow them beyond the grave.

A Christian novelist has other reasons for not losing confidence in himself. I may be attaching too much importance to works of the imagination—the Church has always viewed them with more disdain than fear—but it does seem to me that Grace sometimes makes use of this trouble-stuff, these quite feeble poisons. It is not just a silly notion of mine; I could cite various cases to support it if they did not too intimately involve private experiences of other people. One person whose insight and suffering enabled her to help many people, confided to a novelist that his books had given her the knowledge of evil she needed to reach some sinners and to understand the secret of their wretched lives. The theoretical knowledge of vice and passion handed out to seminary students would have alienated her rather than helped her to help others. But the novelist, without rubbing her nose in human depravity, guided her through the shadowy world inhabited by the ravaged and the possessed. The people she had seen flounder through fictitious lives she recognized by a cry or a glance in their counterparts in the world of actuality. In this way one heroic, saintly spirit benefited from the sad experience of a teller of tales.

To this the theologian will retort that even if Grace makes use of evil for a greater good, the evil is not excused or made legitimate thereby. The Christian studies and observes his passions only to conquer them; he lingers over them only so long as he must in order to win his victory over them. We flatter ourselves (he would say) that a faithful, accurate picture portraying the horror of sin is therefore inoffensive. Passion being what it is, has the unveiling of its shame and unhappy consequences ever persuaded anyone to give it up? If it is true, so bitterly true as to be almost inadmissible, that we never commit a wrong action, even against our will, without longing sooner or later to commit it again (after all, habit begins with the first act), then even the unpitying delineation of grave human aberrations makes us, through the power of the imagination, accomplices in evil. It may even incite us to more concrete experience, because the image itself can become an enticement, drawing us from the familiar into the habitual.

One novel only, one play only, is offered to the Christian: his own. This is the story of the struggle that is played out between him and his Creator. The only purpose of giving this literary form could be to attract

and beguile the reader. Yet I trust that my opponents
will not be too quick to snatch up the weapons I am
putting at their disposal. What shocks me in an otherwise excellent periodical like the *Revue des lectures* of
Father Béthléem is not so much what it condemns as
what it recommends. I would agree if, with Port-Royal
and Saint-Sulpice, with Bossuet and even Fénelon, it
had the courage to reject all creative literature; but instead of doing that, it defends one of the worst kinds—
the only kind, I believe, that has no justification what-
soever. A faithful portrait of man may be dangerous,
but at least it has the merit of being faithful. Thanks to
such honesty, Grace finds a way to take possession of
the ambiguous but truthful work and make it serve its
own ends. Those novels of mine that have elicited the
loudest outcries have, I am assured, given direction to
some people. But a falsification of reality, an untrue
portrait of man is absolutely bad and serves only the
demon of witless stupidity, the fiend who sometimes
opens the half-latched door to all his fellow devils.

And, by way of further example, it calls for con-
siderable virtue on my part to be pleased with the
blurb for my play *Asmodée* in the *Revue des lectures:*
"For the instructed adult who, for whatever reason
(peace in the family, for example), cannot, in a given
situation, avoid going to the theater . . ."

There is an obscenity based on trivialities and lies
that is perhaps worse than the other, because it attacks
young Christian girls exclusively. What a travesty that
the possession of Christian truth condemns our chil-

dren, and only them, to an inferior diet of degrading platitudes!

Could we not prepare at least substantial foods for these young people? Nothing is less colorless than virtue, actually, and the search for holiness will always be man's greatest adventure. But it's a long way from hagiography to the novel. We can write the life of a saint, if we are of a mind to do so, but it is impossible to imagine writing a novel about a saint, that is, creating a saint: Grace is not invented. Bernanos is the only man who has known how to create all those martyrized priests of his from his own substance, without borrowing anything from hagiography. But precisely because he is a novelist and not a biographer, their cross is always rooted in muck. I don't know what the *Revue des lectures* thought of Mouchette and the disturbing faun crouching in *L'Imposture,* but it is quite evident that the one novelist whose theme is saintliness is as involved as any one of us in the refuse of the world. He nails his country priest to a scaffold outlined against shadows swollen with crime.

I have sometimes wondered what kind of book would be written by a young man who had deliberately elected to become a saint. Duhamel has created his unforgettable Salavin, but Salavin evolves outside the Church. I am thinking rather of a spirit that aspires to model itself after Christ by following methods consecrated by the experience of the great mystics. It seems to me that if the novelist passed beyond appearances and penetrated profoundly into the inner man, he could not possibly avoid portraying a fallen nature, but he would touch on a less familiar guise of evil. He would be writing a story of masked passions, which his hero, enamored of his own perfection, would not recognize. Sensuality, which cannot be disguised, he would dominate and conquer. But he would never recognize the faces of other capital sins, especially of pride, because they would have contrived to assume an edifying aspect for him, and would outdo themselves in ardor and zeal until their victim considered himself a god. Perhaps the true saint is the man who does not stop at every instant to unmask and to verify all the veiled passions within him. Whence the humility, the abysses of humility, that impress us so in those who have already won a place in Heaven. For they see what we do not see; they know that throughout their lives they had constantly to snatch knife and mask from the vices that disguise themselves as virtues.

THOUGHTS IN THE JUNGLE

It is easier to bear some abuse if I reflect, "I do not deserve this reproach, but I do deserve others that have not been made." There is however a debit column known only to myself, one in which I enter acts of perfidy that astound even more than they disturb me. In this latter sense, I do indeed merit every reproach.

My enemies sometimes write about me more truly than they know, the truth, however, being on a plane

they are not aware of. It is curious to watch them re-
connoiter a point of attack often far removed from the
actual center of conflict. My writing seems to them confused and dangerous, especially since I have been making a great effort to judge certain events impartially
and with an open mind. In their eyes, this means that
I have become a man who doesn't "abide by the rules
of the game." I am breaking the unwritten law that
unites people of a given caste or world. And if I do
not mend my ways, I will soon become a man against
whom no holds are barred.

These people do not believe they are unjust. To their
way of thinking, I am the member of a privileged group
and therefore must not play the game of those who are
fighting privilege. This is the law of the jungle in our
world, and it has some justification. But in the ex-
tremity of his prosperity, can the prisoner crying
through the bars of his gilded cage not recall a few
facts?

Can he not recollect, for example, that the last word
almost always lies with the "haves"? The property instinct always prevails over the rage and revolt of the
"have-nots." The man who possesses a treasure lives
cautiously and almost always holds the top cards. Or
can he remember that the anger of the poor is quick to
subside? The politicians of the Left exploit it and
dictate how it shall be expressed. Poverty thus becomes
grist for many rival mills. Or can he recall that a well-
behaved little boy will suddenly snarl and glower like

an animal that thinks its bone is threatened? Or does
he remember the message of Bernanos: nothing is dis-
tributed more evenly in this world than cruelty?

THE PRIDE OF POETS

The poet's pride is only a defense; self-doubt corrodes the greatest among them. They need our testimony if they are not to despair. Nightingale in the
spring, skylark, cicada that bursts into song and cradles
a drowsy world, cricket wintering among the ashes of
a hearth—the poet is never sure that he has been heard.
His song spirals among the stars to plummet on his own
heart.

He feels that it is a betrayal or an act of cowardice
for us to be silent. Silence is so easy. And the day is
long past when the Muse needed no help to make her
way among men. Who still speaks the dead language of
poetry? The last of the young people to be as mad for
poetry as we were at their age have been destroyed by
the surrealist plague.

The poet who climbs upon a soapbox to shout, "I
am a genius!" does not deserve to be reproached for
this but we do so deserve for not having been able to
give him confidence, especially when our disregard follows on years of adulation. After the First World War,
Mme. de Noailles died, suffocated by the empty air,
like a queen whose palace is deserted when the enemy

approaches; it is always indifference and oblivion that assassinate the poet.

If suffering sometimes leads poets to excess, let us accept their reproach, mindful of the rights they have over us. For most men are born deaf and blind; the poet appears, catches up a bit of pure mud from the bottom of the spring, touches our eyelids and our ears and, suddenly, we see and we hear. Long ago Francis Jammes opened my eyes in this way to the beauty of the world.

The sight of an inspired poet first annoys a Frenchman; then he turns self-righteous and instinctively picks up a stone. Yet among all the things of this world, nothing is left to believe in except poetry and music. The grandeur of man lies in song, not in thought. Thoughts mislead and lie. Our opponent is always right on one point or another. What reasoning is not banal? Even in the realm of science, what theory does not wear out or become null? Nothing is forever true except that which is inspired. One cannot, for example, imagine a verse of Racine's ever turning false. So long as men exist on the face of the earth, some measures of Mozart will testify to our innocence, lost from the beginning and yet existing somewhere, since we hear it laughing and crying in his heavenly music.

But it is hard to be musician or poet and not to hope for one's own survival. Francis Jammes was granted the great grace that his faith in God re-enforced his faith in himself. He believed that his genius was disclosing one ray of eternal beauty once and for all time.

And he was right to believe this; the stream that flows under the alders of his poems springs from the divine source; the flowers that perfume his poems, the self-same cowslips and lilacs, can lay claim to immortal names.

Jammes was annoyed that the critics did not do him justice. But he knew, with a sure knowledge, that he was a great poet; this is a happiness not granted to many. Most writers (I know of at least one) are bitterly certain that they will die twice—first, in their bodies and, secondly, in their books. They feel themselves condemned to a double dust, a double death. I often think of the faces that will fade, little by little, from the pages of my novels and of all those eyes that no hand will ever close.

ART AND THE PUBLIC

Very few authors know how to write for children because most of them have concocted an absurd idea of what childhood is. And they have done the same in relation to the adult public. In a democracy, this public has its worshipers who treat it as some kind of puerile deity that they assume understands nothing about anything. Accordingly, playwrights fabricate garishly melodramatic situations intended to appeal to the passions they ascribe to the public—passions which are precisely those that the audience checks (together with its hat and coat) when it enters the theater.

A mass audience as such does not exist for the theater, unless it be the audience to which we all belong. Shakespeare, Corneille, Racine, Molière, and de Musset create a brief equality of tears and laughter among all of us. For tears and laughter are not the privilege of any one class, the only difference being that ordinary people give in to them more readily than do sophisticates and are less prone to throw up defenses against outside opinion.

When I was eighteen I used to go to the Grand-Théâtre in Bordeaux, and the stamping and cheering that *Traviata* elicited from the gallery would make me smile and shrug. In retrospect, I consider that I was a blockhead and that the peanut-gallery patrons were right to let themselves go in response to such ravishing music.

I am suspicious of a play that is beyond the grasp of the general run of people, for the public is always equal to any theater masterpiece. I feel the same way about books. I would not want to swear that a writer finds many more responsive readers among the middle classes than in the others. Nevertheless, our female readers from the upper reaches of society are fewer than we flatter ourselves or than they would like us to believe. I know an author who was helping sell his own books recently at a charity affair. He enjoyed himself no end watching how some women would glance quickly away as they hurried by his wares; they looked exactly like indifferent, mistrustful dogs being offered a tangerine.

An author need only publish a book that, for some extra-literary reason, travels beyond the magic circle of the sixty thousand regular readers of "the best-selling novelists" (as they say when they want to get under our skin). Then he realizes how many people there are who are not illiterate, but for whom the bookshop does not exist. I have received several very correct letters requesting me to mail my *Vie de Jésus* collect. It never occurred to my correspondents to go to a bookshop for it. They had probably never been in one in their whole lives.

People who are concerned with their own emotions and search in our books for some reflection of them live in a small city that is not found on any map. But this is the public for which we work, a public comprising students, middle-class wives, teachers, curates, taxi drivers, and duchesses. These readers do not want us to describe people from their own circles and are all the more interested in our characters because they do not meet such people in their everyday life. Of course, they want primarily to discover themselves in our pages, but they also want to meet people who are different.

To come back to the theater: people have had instilled in them a horror of their country's past and a scorn for its history and religion, and they have been brought up from infancy to hate inherited or acquired privilege. If the public had not been so conditioned, it would be able to share through the theater the communion that the Greeks knew, that every civilization can achieve if the things that bind the people together have not been furiously hunted down and attacked. Within an old democracy, a simple human verity experienced simultaneously from the boxes to the gallery suffices to create this unity throughout a whole audience; the most corrupt politics cannot erode this unshakable foundation. In our society where so many other values are declining, the miraculous youthfulness of the great classics shines like a beacon; they gain from the collapse of all the rest.

THE ADVENT OF A RUSSIAN PROUST

I was once dismayed to read, in the *Echo de Paris,* the reply of my dear colleague and friend Tharaud to the attacks of Karl Radek against bourgeois literature. Tharaud surrendered the whole argument to his opponent with one simple sentence: "Proust has often insisted on writing in minute detail about fashionable idlers of unqualified mediocrity who become entangled in adventures that are as inconsequential as they themselves and do not deserve to be recounted." This sentence robbed of much of their import very pertinent objections that Tharaud made elsewhere.

The Bolsheviks are reviving the eternal confusion between people's social and moral value and the human interest they hold for the novelist. This warning bell used to be sounded by the so-called right-thinking elements, and, all in all, it is agreeable to find such simple-mindedness equitably divided, thanks to Bolshevism, between the Right and the Left.

There is a kind of reverse snobbism which compels us to deny that any human being *above* a certain social level can be at all interesting. Yet any human creature, simply by virtue of being in this world and of breathing, feeling, loving, hating—whether under the paneled ceilings of the Hôtel de Guermantes, in the bedroom of Odette Swann, in the shadows of Grandet's kitchen, or in the Yonville house where Emma Bovary eats out her heart—can call a masterpiece into being. How dismal it is to live in a period when one must repeat these fundamental truths every day!

Tharaud went so far as to grant Radek that people should interest the artist only to the extent that they stand out from the human collectivity. "For example," said Radek, "Henry Deterding, the petroleum king, is a worth-while subject only when he is engaged in his battle with Standard Oil or the Soviet Union. . . ." And Tharaud approved: "This seems right to me. . . ."

It seemed right to him! Naturally, if we are writing a novel about a man like Henry Deterding, we will portray him *also* in his professional life; the links between his professional and his inner or, simply, his human life, and the conflicts that these may create are the true subject of the novel or the play. When Racine was studying the passions of a Titus or a Nero, he thought the same thing. Show men only in the official or public acts of their existence? One might as well spend one's time costuming puppets. Radek could do as well to propose the Musée Grévin as an example to the sculptors of the new Russia.

We understand all too well why Gogol, Tolstoy, Turgenev, and Dostoevski do not have among them one heir in a country that was once in the vanguard of European literature. But if this heir is born some day, if some seed of Russian genius has been able to germinate outside the Soviet hothouses, if it manages to bloom, to produce flower and fruit, it will not be what Radek imagined.

A Balzac or a Proust arrived at the individual human being through the society of his period. Every social estate, even the proletarian, creates a society. We do not know what kind of society is being built today in the Soviet Union. *Until it produces a great novelist, we shall not know.* For only the evidence of the novelists carries weight. All the tourists have misled us. They have seen nothing, they have only looked. They report to us on appearances, but they have not discovered what lies within.

Man cannot be made over. A political or social revolution modifies him, but it does not make him over. I salute the unknown Proust who may be living today in some remote city in Russia, where he studies the inner life of his people of whom we know nothing except that they suffer cruelly. Everything that is not official, not approved, interests this nameless Proust. Nothing is too base for him, no type of human being seems to him too mediocre; every experience is worthy of being reported to the extent that it is humanly revealing. He is there, secretly garnering the vast harvest of all that Radek scorns, and one day he will render unto Soviet Russia what Soviet Russia will unintentionally have loaned him. He will offer the true face of Russia to the world.

Nothing spontaneous will be alien to this still unborn novelist. He despises slogans only. Attitudes interest him as attitudes, masks as masks. And perhaps he has already jotted down on the margin of his manuscript the golden rule that André Gide gives us on the opening page of *L'Immoraliste:* "I have not tried to prove anything, but I have tried to paint well and to light my painting well."

2. *And on Writers*

GIDE'S JOURNAL

In his *Journal,* Gide quotes a young man who is dying: "It's no fun to play in a world where everybody cheats." These words arouse our pity because they bespeak such dreadful disillusionment. But they also touch us to the quick. We glance at our own hands and examine the dice we are shaking. Are they loaded? Are we all cheats? Do we only pretend to believe what we say we believe? Do we take from the world and from our own selves only what serves our own ends and reenforces our own prejudices?

Gide never doubted this for a moment, hence his irritation with Maurice Barrès. According to Gide, Barrès was strongly drawn to the East but denied his deepest impulses and manufactured false gods—the earth and the dead. We no longer need be much concerned with Barrès's doctrine, the inadequacies of which are only too apparent, but rather with Barrès's

constant effort to surpass his own limitations. The need
grew more insistent every day; he was not sufficient unto himself. He would have been a cheat, actually, had
he not always been mindful of just such a possibility.
Barrès never denied, much less did he try to destroy,
his taste for illusion and the distintegration of the self;
he aspired only to remain in control of it. He made a
place in his life for escape, he allowed himself
breathers. "It's a question of my finally doing something to please myself after holding the reins so tight
for so long," he wrote in the spring of 1914, just before
he left for the Orient. But he had no sooner dropped
the reins than he pulled himself up short. Or rather,
the exigencies of another aspect of his nature made
themselves felt: "I am not going in search of color or
imagery but to enrich my spirit," he wrote.

Barrès, at best only a wishful Christian, should have
been anything but annoying to Gide. Gide should have
found him appealing because he never sacrificed one
of his inner conflicts for the sake of harmony and yet
he somehow managed to orchestrate the dissident voices
within him. In other words, Barrès succeeded where
Gide failed. He was always able to give us the entirety
of himself.

Barrès spent his whole life keeping himself in tune,
as it were. Gide, on the other hand, established himself
in discord; he was torn by conflict and for a long time
reduced to the debate between Christian and Greek.
These two opponents in his heart took turns in speaking their pieces, and sometimes lapsed into fuzzy argu-

ment. But he never stopped being divided within himself. True, early in his life he took a stand in favor of the spontaneous, free flowering of the instinctual life, but this was before he was able to bring himself around to jettisoning that part of himself that had always protested. Sometimes, as in *Numquid et tu,* its low, inarticulate groan drowned the voice of the sensual man.

Around 1932 all protests seemed to have been smothered; Gide appeared to have shaken off something or someone. And what he wrote from then on weighed less; it grew terribly light. Was this achieved by cheating? Who can say? One way to cheat is to slip a card from one's sleeve. Gide has not done this, but there is a card missing from his game, the card inscribed with the Name that is above all other names has disappeared, and in its place he has substituted another (how soiled and finger-marked it is!), which bears one word: Progress. "I should like to live long enough," he wrote, "to see the Russian Plan succeed. . . . I applaud this gigantic and humane undertaking with all my heart." The André Gide who taught us when we were young that we are each unique and irreplaceable longed for the triumph of the Bolshevik anthill in which all creatures are interchangeable.

Even at the cost of playing into my adversary's hand, I must concede that if death had not halted Barrès on his march toward Catholicism, he would have had to give up this very human and beautiful orchestration of the conflicting voices of his soul. He would have had to choose, he would have had to retrench, he would have had to throw some of his booty overboard. Does to choose mean to cheat? If choosing is cheating, then everyone cheats, including the man who chooses not to choose. And the young man whose terrible dying words Gide reported did well to die.

Gide would protest that he, at least, does not cheat; he sacrificed what he received from outside influences, what education forced on him. He preserved what truly belonged to him and was a part of his deepest nature. The Christian turns this claim against him, saying that what survived was his desire for purity and perfection. It is an endless debate, and what referee can ever give a dicision that will stand? Perhaps Gide believed he could. In his last *Journal* he wrote: "In my own experience, I have often seen how often an obligation, a thing that must be done, has given me a feeling of happiness. I will not manage to win complete possession of myself without discipline. Here is where religion wins out. A thinking human being who has no purpose outside himself suffers from an abominable emptiness. The voyage through life is only a distraction for him. I am now of an age when I should like to demand the best of myself. But I have forgotten how to do it and am getting nothing."

Let us not rejoice too soon in our debate with Gide. If religious observance is only a discipline that even a Gide now and then feels the lack of, what reason would there be to remain faithful to it? It is not a discipline pure and simple that we need; we need love. If the yoke we accept were not one of love, who would endure it? This is something that Barrès, an offspring of Renan, surely did not grasp, whereas Gide understood very well what it means. For the Christian it is not a question of throwing up barriers or battlements, or of outfitting himself with crutches. A man who tries to live by Christian law is simply showing that *he prefers Someone*. He may love many other things, he may be responsive to the appeal of a very different life, may understand Montaigne and Nietzsche, but there is Someone in his life whom he prefers even if he sometimes betrays Him. This is a personal affair between another being and ourselves. It is an endless debate in which we sometimes arm ourselves against Christ with the arguments of humanism, at other times with something else, but we always have to come round, in Claudel's words, "like a man who prefers his friend."

This is no construction of the mind, no fantasy. Someone has truly come, certain words have been said, certain promises have been made. "And," Gide insinuated in his *Journal,* "if the pearl of great price, which a man gives all his wealth to possess, turns out to be a false pearl?" Barrès might have answered, "What do I care? Catholicism has earthly value and that is enough. It nourishes the spirit, it creates beauty. . . ."

On this point, I feel closer to Gide. For if I believed that the pearl was false, no matter how I might benefit from it, I would cast it away with rage. But here the Grace of God and the virtue of man—Faith followed by Hope—intervene.

This morning I attended a ceremony in which a

young Benedictine novice was taking his vows. At a certain moment he raised both arms and intoned three times, in Latin, on a rising note of ardent supplication: "May I not be mistaken in my trust!" There was no pain in this prayer. If a particle of anguish did survive, a wave of love and joy sprang from his innermost pure heart to cover it. Love, true love, carries within itself its own certitude.

II

Gide was annoyed—and rightly—when he was reproached for being both a rich man and a Communist. But why did he, then, deliver the same kind of below-the-belt blow to Catholics? And especially why, challenging one's right to call himself a Christian, did he bring up the Biblical story of the rich young man but quote only Christ's final words in the narrative?

The rich young man asked Christ what he must do to win everlasting life, and Christ enumerated the commandments: "Thou shalt not kill. Thou shalt not commit adultery. Thou shalt not steal. Thou shalt not bear false witness. Honor thy father and thy mother. And, thou shalt love thy neighbor as thyself." And He said no more, as if He had spelled out His requirements in full: these after all are the things God wants from the ordinary man. And they are not so negligible, either. Love one's neighbor as oneself? That is perfection indeed!

But the young man does not cut their conversation short. He summons up his courage: "All these I have kept ever since I was a child. What is yet wanting to me?" He is surrendering to some attraction, aspiring to something more. "And Jesus, looking upon him, loved him." Nothing has changed since that was said. All of us are loved, but there are the few whom Jesus looks at suddenly and whom He loves with the love that demands the total gift of self: "If thou wilt be perfect, go, sell what thou hast, and give to the poor . . . and come, follow me."

We ask Gide: Since the day when these words were pronounced, has Christian life not followed the pattern Christ demanded? Through the centuries, how many human beings have renewed Saint Francis's espousal of poverty! Not only humble men but even a Pascal, who wrote "I love poverty because Christ loved it." This, it seems to me, is a very telling remark.

Christ does not insist that those nearest Him *be* poor but rather that they *choose* to be poor. This is why the most austere orders are recruited, in part, from among the rich. My opponent would retort that this merely proves why capitalism finds it advantageous to promote religious observance among the working classes. (Gide was particularly partial to this polemical charge.) The Christian's duty is indeed to seek justice first and, by extension, to work to remedy social injustice, never to resign himself to it. (Gide was obviously unaware of the social doctrine of the Church and of the importance of Christian syndicalism throughout the world.)

Yet in a parallel way, the true Christian strives to instill in himself and in others the spirit of proverty,

of detachment. Today individuals and nations aspire—
wrongly—to a false wealth. Who can be sure that our
modern enslavement to the machine and to material
well-being does not represent the ultimate in the
wealth-mindedness that Christ excoriated? The Church
simultaneously battles against material suffering and
preaches the ideal of poverty. Such is its paradox; it
multiplies its charitable works and still exhorts more
and more men to follow Christ in poverty; it peoples
the earth with stripped hearts.

You can always argue against the exploitation of
Christ by the rich by saying that the great financiers of
the Left exploit socialism and democracy just as cyni-
cally. But their worst crime is to make themselves our
accomplices in compromising religion and to supply
us with an argument for defrauding the poor of union
with God. For let us confess that our love of wealth is
the token that we ourselves have not taken the first step
on the side of God. Even in those who have taken the
vow of poverty this love often reappears, masked in one
way or another. Ambition apart, it is unquestionably
the most insidious of all our drives.

The rapid climb to success, the seemingly uncal-
culated ease with which a man manages always to pre-
empt first place, this is a significant sign which no
honest man can disavow when he detects it in his own
life. But suppose that we have none of the rough-shod
ambition that prevails most widely today, and have
always—and in perfect sincerity—professed ourselves indifferent to preferment. Let us then have the courage

to recognize that success is the measure of real ambition, ambition that is shrewd enough to be blind. The
indiscretions, the expansiveness, the reckless abandon,
the protestations of faith, the impulse to rebel—is this
ostensible excess not characteristic behavior in the man
who, knowing that all calculation is thwarted by reality,
trusts to his instinct, the instinct of the mule on the
mountain that plods peacefully along the outer edge
of the abyss?

In man, the instinct of self-preservation expands and
flowers into the instinct of self-advancement, which op-
erates with amazing sureness. Once success has been
achieved, this instinct is, furthermore, quite compatible
with a kind of detachment. Achieve everything, not in
order to enjoy it but to be able to ignore it—this is a
method some Christians use to cure themselves of ambition. They no longer think of themselves as ambitious
once they have outgrown their awareness of having attained high estate. But the process of winning worldly
honors without undue effort and without intrigue so
that we have no pretext for being diverted from the
"single necessity"—no saint, to my knowledge, has ever
followed this road to reach God. Did Bossuet, or
Fénelon, or even Lacordaire?

Here, if I may put it so, we achieve that junction of
the righteous life and material well-being where
Pharisaism (especially a kind that can be found in
Anglo-Saxon Protestantism) reaps its returns. Does God
reward His servants here below with material advantages? A life that is honorable in men's eyes is almost

inevitably a life replete with success, but let us spare ourselves the mockery of foisting upon the God whose wounded body hangs suspended by three nails on a gallows a share in any such distribution of prizes. Let us simply recognize the fact that between an honorable life and honors there exists the relation of cause and effect.

Let us dare to go further: this instinct of self-advancement, which is constantly in play and functions the more surely because we are not often fully aware of it, was also operative when we chose to set out on a definite path. To what extent was this instinct the determining factor? There are many other motives, as we know, and we have analyzed them a thousand times. But this secret motion of the self that seeks its own advantage is diffused through all our thoughts, it slips into our most casual words, is stranger to none of our silences, governs our likes and dislikes, and it reveals immense resources of patience in those who are the most irritable, the least fashioned for enduring the importunate or the stupid. We never know exactly what share of the solemn decisions that determine our destiny must be attributed to it.

Those of us who realize that no part of us is free of corruption should not be troubled by this; Grace prunes away the rottenness. Yet what a play Molière would have written if he had not made Tartufe clearly aware of his hypocrisy! A half-sincere Tartufe would have been sublimely true and, as a consequence, abominably comic. The true Christian cannot resemble Molière's

impostor even remotely, but he must keep the image
of the half-sincere Tartufe before his eyes in order to
be on his guard. Actually, the rationalist who does not
live in the presence of God risks being far closer to
Tartufe than does the believing man. He, like Tartufe
is forever adjusting *his* god, which is human Reason, to
the demands of his feelings. It is laughable to watch our
humanists cutting the cloth of their principles to measure. As they see it, it becomes a man's duty from one
day to the next to leave his wife, to take the wife of
another, to gratify this or that inclination. Tartufe is
to be found in them more often than in us, because
compromises can always be made with man but never
with Heaven.

III

Many French workers were turning their backs on
Moscow, but Moscow found great consolation among
the élite. Moscow held a charm for various extremely
sensitive and subtle writers, first among them, André
Gide, whom the Five-Year Plan plunged into an altogether remarkable delirium. His delirium differed,
however, from the Bolshevik fervor of assorted members of the upper classes whose case was more simple:
having gorged themselves on all that could be had for
money, those society luminaries aspired only to the
gratuitous luxury of a priggish, impertinent posturing
that cost them nothing. But it was delightful to observe
them when the question of their marrying or of marrying off their children came up. Did they look for al-

liances with the extreme Left? Of course not. These
fashionable Bolsheviks fell over themselves in their
hurry to snag the best name and the biggest fortune
available. And if they had to settle for something less
on the first score, when it came to money they did not
compromise.

When the literary élite turned to Moscow, however,
it was succumbing to a deeper appeal. Those people
were also laden with all the advantages of a great and
solid fortune; they had lived a secure, sheltered life
surrounded by the delights of culture. But perhaps they
suffered secretly from a bad conscience? Let us at least
concede that they knew the torments of the hunger and
thirst for justice that Christ instills in the heart of every
man born into this world, for it would be unjust to
claim that the crisis gripping them was devoid of all
nobility. But a hunger and thirst for justice would not
have sufficed to enamor them of Bolshevism initially;
it would have quickly alienated them. I think their motives were less elevated.

It used to be that my youngest child could not catch
sight of an Indonesian friend of mine without hurling
himself into the man's arms. "Is that because you love
him so much?" I asked. "Oh, no!" he answered. "He
scares me so. . . ." The fascination exercised over some
of our best minds might not have been very different
in kind. I recall those early drawings by Jean Cocteau
in *Potomak,* in which the respectable Mortimer
ménage was fascinated by some monsters called Eugène.
The clutch of Moscow-bound intellectuals, great lit-

erary bourgeois that they were, dressed like first-class travelers and armed with elegant luggage from Barnabooth, approached the Bolshevik ogre with measured tread and deep salaams, offering it paeans of praise that at least helped us in part to see through their peculiar adventure. They professed to be attracted to Communism first and foremost by their love of Progress; this is an article of faith with them and does not admit discussion. It would have ill become us to press this point, for one must always take off from an act of faith, even if Gide picked up the remark of a Reverend Father, "There are immutable principles with reference to which doubt is not permissible," only to add that a more vacuous and "more stupidly sonorous" phrase could not be imagined. But Gide, however, did not permit us to question (1) that humanity was progressing, and (2) that this progress was uniquely manifest in Bolshevism.

His conviction extended so far as to let him find it good that this forward march "shakes some good souls up a bit." He was of course referring to Russian Christians. He did not want to hear of their having been persecuted, and even spoke lightly of this, using the tone massacres always inspire in a certain type of decent person. "Was the blood that has been shed so pure, after all?" a Girondist exclaimed amiably the day after the September butchery. André Gide (who had the audacity to insist that religion alone, or almost alone, practices persecution) did not go so far as his great predecessor; he simply denied the existence of any martyrs of Russian Orthodoxy. According to him, nothing was done to them except that their priests were forbidden to "knead the minds of children," as he dared put it.

But let us suspend the debate and, together with the good father whom Gide made fun of, confess that immutable principles do exist. There is one in particular that I should like to express as simply as I can: Each of us knows that he could become less evil than he is. There is no man living who does not know for a certainty that he has within him the power to become better. And let no one object that "better" is open to definition. I say again: There is no one in this world who does not see, or who, at least, has not seen, very clearly where he must master himself in order to become, not a saint, perhaps, but a good man in the highest sense of the word. I say categorically that this awareness is so deeply rooted in us that we have great difficulty in eradicating it. It took Gide half a century—not a day less—to uproot his clear view of inner progress and substitute for it his naïve faith in materialistic progress.

Let us drop here the controversial point of whether humanity is following an upward path. The question is, in any case, one of hope and not of certainty. Some men believe in this "progress" with a fervor that is in direct proportion to the passion they have used to destroy within themselves the bar of conscience that judges all crimes. The human progress they applaud beguiles them particularly because they anticipate that it will bring about a reversal of values similar to that which they have tried to achieve in themselves. They have a deep self-interest in confounding progress with their personal disorder; they must do so if they are to pass by unnoticed. They hope not to die before saluting the new dawn when the moral order they flout and deny will no longer be inscribed in the tradition of man. *This new society,* they say, *in which the mind and heart of children will have been so thoroughly kneaded that they will have lost all ability to distinguish between good and evil—may it be born quickly.* What an admirable aspiration for these great intellects—a new society in which no one will be obliged to feel remorse since even the names of vice will be forgotten! "I should like to shout aloud my sympathy with the U.S.S.R.," cried M. Gide, in the *Nouvelle Revue Française,* "and have my cry be heard far and wide! I should like to live long enough to see this tremendous effort succeed. I hope with all my heart that it will triumph and I wish that I could work for it. I wish that I could live to see what a state without religion, a society without cloisters, can produce. Religion and the family are the two worst enemies of Progress."

Religion, the family: where could inner progress find greater support? Yet this progress is not only different from what Gide considered the general progress of humanity; it is inimical to it. We can now see clearly that it would have been futile to try to prove to that neophyte that the Bolshevik dictatorship is one of the most crushing that mankind has ever endured. What did external coercion matter to him? The one restraint that he feared was the moral law that, working against our natures, strengthens religion and the family. That law, he thought, had been vanquished and the victory could not be too dearly paid. He believed there was a place in this world where man, no matter what he did, could not commit evil since good and evil were suppressed by fiat. What a miracle that would be!

The inner progress of man according to Christ, material progress according to Marxism: we keep coming back to these two cities, raised against each other throughout time. I for my part have faith in the one that appears to be the weaker.

"There are days," Gide wrote, "when, if only I let myself go, I would roll right under the Communion table. . . ." Only the feeling of Gide should concern us here, not the grossness of the phrase; he added that it was intellectual honesty that restrained him, but I believe, with Bourdaloue, "that whether we have or do not have this light does not depend on us. . . ." For there are men who will be enlightened and who will be called, indefatigably, to the end.

MAURICE DE GUÉRIN

A hundred years after a man has returned to dust, he scarcely cares whether he is admired or not, but it matters to him greatly that he be loved. Beside Lamartine or Hugo, Maurice de Guérin rather resembles some poor boy whose school notebooks have been discovered at the bottom of his desk, and yet he is the one privileged to keep a place in our hearts and, if we have a faith, in our prayers. For my part, he is the one friend from my youth whom I have not lost and whom I can now be sure I shall never lose.

When I was twenty, I had a predilection for the group of intense young men, both laymen and priests, who thronged around Father Lamennais at La Chênaie. Maurice de Guérin seemed quite lost among them. Today Montalembert and even Lacordaire himself mean very little to me. I have turned away from those all too eloquent lips; the longer I live, the more I have come to prefer the quiet ones.

At La Chênaie, Maurice was the one man who did not talk. Neither M. Féli nor Lacordaire thought very highly of the taciturn young fellow. But how surprised Lamennais—who fancied himself a prophet—would have been if he could have foreseen that a century later his *Paroles d'un croyant* would carry less weight with us than the private journal of a boy from Languedoc, exiled deep in the gloomy forests of Brittany. Father Lamennais's tragic struggles with Rome absorb us less today than the conflicts hidden in the heart of Maurice de Guérin, conflicts from which he unburdened himself, at night, by recording his thoughts and impressions in a little green notebook.

What conflicts? What is the drama of Maurice de Guérin? Perhaps to understand it profoundly one must have lived it, from childhood have been as he, touched

by Grace and captivated by the gods. Everyone ought
to know by heart these famous lines of his: I treasure
them above all others.

Comme un fruit suspendu dans l'ombre du feuillage,
Mon destin s'est formé dans l'épaisseur des bois.
J'ai grandi, recouvert d'une chaleur sauvage,
Et le vent qui rompait le tissu de l'ombrage
Me découvrit le ciel pour la première fois.
Les faveurs de nos dieux m'ont touché dès l'enfance:

Mes plus jeunes regards ont aimé les forêts,
Et mes plus jeunes pas ont suivi le silence
Qui m'entraînait bien loin dans l'ombre et les secrets.
Mais le jour où, du haut d'une cime perdue,
Je vis (ce fut pour moi comme un brillant réveil!)
Le monde parcouru par les feux du soleil,
Et les champs et les eaux couchés dans l'étendue
L'étendue enivra mon esprit et mes yeux;
Je voulus égaler mes regards à l'espace,
Et posséder sans borne en égarant ma trace,
L'ouverture des champs avec celle des cieux.

The mystery of Guérin is expressed in these few
lines. Those who do not belong to his spiritual race
can admire the gifted stylist of *Bacchante* and *Centaure,*
but they could never reach the heart of the mystery
I speak of. The crowd of trees means more to Guérin
than the crowd of men. Lacordaire and Montalembert
addressed great auditoriums resounding with shouts
and applause, but Guérin traffics only with the motionless, mute beings whose leafy crowns are stirred by the
wind and whose bark conceals unknown passions.

Probably he did love some human beings, or at least

thought he did. The Baronne de Maistre received deathless love letters from him. And yet, it has always seemed to me that through the eyes of this mortal woman, Cybele stared fixedly at her wild child and drew him out into the night where tossing boughs clashed in the wind.

Perhaps no one found so profound a place in his heart as the young wife of his friend Hippolyte de la Morvonnais, the Marie to whom he never addressed one word of love. But he had lived near her in the Val d'Arguenon, by the cradling sea; one evening, when he had to go away, she murmured from the steps a last farewell that was lost in the dark, squalling night. Henceforth, Marie, who was dying, would be fused in his memory with the upward sweep of the constellations and with the foam and the whisperings of the tides. She would be blended with the immobility and the silence of the night, as he listened to the throb of the waves and the whistling wings of the wild ducks. Maurice de Guérin worshiped Marie because he did not separate her in any way from a universe he worshiped.

The fascination of the natural world of creation not only turned Maurice de Guérin from human creatures but from the Uncreated, from God. It was almost always the disappointment and profound irritation that an indifferent Nature aroused in the romantics that threw them back on God. Maurice de Guérin knew no such feelings. He would never have said reproachfully, with Olympio, *"Nature au front serein, comme vous oubliez!"* Nothing would have been more alien to him than de Vigny's imprecations and curses on Nature. He would not even have understood them. Being mortal himself, he did not hate Nature for being eternal. All he did was long the more passionately to lose himself, to melt away and perish in her bosom.

Because he felt none of the romantic horror for a blind and deaf Nature, he did not, on the rebound, like so many of his comrades, turn toward the personal God of Christians, the God of Abraham, of Isaac and of Jacob, the gentle and consoling God. He did not search for refuge from mindless matter. From childhood he played between the knees of Cybele and was even then familiar with her copses and springs, her clouds and her mists. He is the eternal Attis, unafraid of Cybele's mysteries, the shepherd, attentive to every breeze, for whom it would be no punishment to find himself one day transformed into a pine tree. "I live with the inner elements of things," he wrote on December 10, 1834. "I swim up paths of light to the stars and up rivers to the heart of the mysteries of their birth. Nature admits me into her most remote dwellings, to that place from which universal life springs. There I discover the cause of all motion and hear the creatures' first song in all its freshness."

Yet Maurice was born a Christian. For years he loved the God whom his sister Eugénie worshiped and possessed in the little church of Andillac: the God who will not share our worship with the heedless goddess.

Can we love both Cybele and Christ? There was a

moment in the world's history, at the dawn of the thirteenth century, when men could believe that Christ —in the person of Francis, the tiny beggar of Assisi— had exorcised Nature. The branches snapped as the last centaur took flight; the saints supplanted the nymphs of the springs; one night a prophetic cry rang out over the sea: "The great Pan is dead!" and at last mankind could believe that what the voice announced had been accomplished. His Brother Sun, the hills, the waves, and the stars around Francis of Assisi sang a hymn of praise to the glory of the Lamb of God. But while the little mendicant with the pierced hands and feet still drew breath, his work was undermined; beneath the bark of the oaks the nymphs awoke, one by one, and the flute of the faun was heard again among the rushes of the pools. Two centuries later came the eruption throughout Nature of gods seen to have been only momentarily dispossessed and conquered; what we call the Renaissance was their revenge.

They returned, but God did not withdraw. He stayed on, dwelling in the wheat and in the wine; every village church held the crucified Lord motionless in its shadows. Around the humble church in Andillac, around the altar with its vessels of worn gilt and the flickering lamp that Eugénie used to tend, the harvests swollen with the blood of Cybele foamed—but they did so in vain. The fields filled the torrid afternoons with a benumbing hum, but this too was in vain. God remained, locked in the embrace of Nature, engulfed within her in a mystery of death and love.

Ever since then the hearts of Christian poets have been divided. Grace and Nature, contending for possession of Maurice de Guérin, transformed his thought into the lightning, which, as he said, "flashes on the horizon between two worlds." Like the centaur, his face reflected the image and likeness of God, but one whole part of his being weltered in the grossest animality.

As his youth slipped away, it was to Cybele that Maurice surrendered. The examination of conscience, the spiritual withdrawal which this young Catholic had practiced from childhood soon became a removal, a flight, a plunge into a delicious abyss where he did not wish to find, but rather to lose, himself.

But to lose oneself is also to work out one's salvation —Eugénie understood these words in their higher, absolute sense. From Le Cayla, where she had put down her roots, she watched her beloved brother move further and further into those spiritual shadows which constitute the light of this world, knowing how terribly adept he was at eluding prayers and exhortations, how inured to dissemblance, defeat, and detours.

For Eugénie, loving Maurice meant loving Maurice's soul. She was obsessed by the fear of being separated from him for all eternity. In the church in Andillac a dialogue went on for years between the humble girl and the modest tabernacle before which she kneeled; between the two of them there was formed a single desire: to save Maurice. From the terrace, from the bedroom where she wrote her journal, she charted his destiny along paths that escaped even her until death came searching for this brother of sorrows in the bedlam of Paris, to lead him home and, on Friday, July 19, 1839, to lay him to sleep at last in the arms of his sister and of his God.

If I had the time, I should like to show precisely how this struggle, this conflict in the soul that is a prey to both Christ and Cybele, inspired a miracle of literature. It created a brief equilibrium such as French prose had perhaps never achieved before and has never found again. From Chateaubriand to Maurice de Guérin, a prose that had turned away from classic perfection passed from flawed adolescence to a maturity of magnificent richness.

More than a hundred years have gone quickly by since Maurice de Guérin's eyes closed on the beauty of this world. But he remains for us the dark-eyed, dark-haired adolescent with the open forehead and pure profile of the last of the Abencérages. He is our youth. He is at once ourselves and the friend we loved; he is the one who escaped the degradation of life through death and who stole from the world and the passions all that God can contemplate without horror. He offers to those of us who love him the image of a nobility and grace unknown to the harsh times in which we are condemned to live.

Visiting Le Cayla today, I look closely at this modest house, this humble kitchen, this living room, this little bedroom, this terrace, this property like all those others where our mothers taught us to pray, to love, and to suffer. It is right to turn them into museums, for the old family estates are threatened with ruin, and the secret of the virtues that were cultivated in their protective shadow seems to be lost—that shadow where even passion and error were imbued with nobility, and resounding to Heaven, were one day redeemed by a sister's immolation.

For me Andillac is a place of meditation, an altar, a living spring where Eugénie came to draw up the secret of sacrifice, this small daily sacrifice that, practiced through the centuries, has peopled France with the unknown saints whose blood flows in our veins. The ashes of this hearth cover the remains of our forgotten dignity. Here the ancient verity that has been repeated a hundred times since Barrès, seems fresh and vital and urgent—and ignored. A civilization is not measured by the speed of travel nor the material comforts of life; like the kingdom of God, it is within us and is bound to a certain spiritual virtue. This virtue is not improvised; it requires the close alliance of generations of men and of God. Centuries of striving for perfection are necessary so that a French family, at a given moment in its obscure history, can suddenly boast a cyme of two fragile, admirable blossoms: Eugénie and Maurice.

Someone may say that, enslaved as we are to an iron law, living in a period when hate rules France and the whole world, we have nothing to do with such almost excessive sensibilities. It's possible. I don't know. But I do know that now and again I still receive a letter from somewhere in a remote province that, were genius also present in it, could have been written from Le Cayla; the tone, if I may say so, is set by what Maurice de Guérin wrote the evening of April 11, 1838 to Barbey d'Aurevilly: "I, who suffer so singularly for the tears of others, overflow with my own tears. A turmoil compounded of pain and delight has taken possession of my spirit. The future that I am entering upon is filled with shadows, the present overwhelms me with good and evil. My heart is strange. Unbelievable conflicts and outpourings of feeling sweep away soul and life and all my strength; the beauty of the day, the potency of air and sun, everything that can distract a feeble mortal surrounds and fills my being. Truly I do not know into how many fragments I should explode, were I at this instant to hear music such as the *Pastoral*. Perhaps God would grant me the Grace of letting whatever makes up my life explode in all directions." And this is how the letter ends: "Adieu! it is a wonderful evening. May the beauty of the night that is drawing near fill you with rapture."

There are still young people whose tears overflow, whose hearts are strange, and who to all appearances are useless, being weak and disarmed in the midst of their ferocious brethren. Yet simply because they exist and because they suffer, they bear witness that the profound spring nourishing the genius of our land is nowhere near exhaustion. For them Le Cayla is henceforth open: they will come to dream before this hallowed horizon that the eyes of Eugénie and Maurice have mirrored. They will come out onto the burning terrace to evoke the shades of brother and sister and to hear in the wind the murmur of their mingled voices.

II

It has often been said that we look in the person we love for the qualities that we ourselves do not possess. Perhaps this is true; perhaps we are never more closely bound to each other than by our differences. But in the case of friends chosen from the past, it is quite the opposite. They resemble us like brothers whom, from book to book, we are eager to discover. When I was a boy, a few lines from Maurice de Guérin's *Journal* could make me feel nearer to him than his Cayla is to my Malagar.

Maurice de Guérin opened my eyes to the beauty of the world, but not, as the great romantics did, to its external beauty; he initiated me into the mute passions of the earth and gave my hesitant, humble adolescence the exhilarating certainty that I was the consciousness of inanimate nature. Trees tormented by the east wind, hills swept by the shadows of clouds acquired awareness in me; in and through me, I believed, Nature came to know God and not only adored Him but united with Him in the Eucharist—what Guérin splendidly called "the rendezvous of God and all creation in mankind."

Was it chance that the friends I loved most—André Lafon, Jean de la Ville de Mirmont—seemed to have inherited some part of the secret that charmed Maurice de Guérin into immobility as, at dusk, the birds passed over his head, seeking a resting place for the night?

André Lafon once compared himself to a statue, and did not know that Maurice de Guérin had used the same image when, one night on a promontory of the Val d'Argunon, he gave no sign of life except to raise his head to the whistling of the wild ducks' wings.

But, as my friends vanished, they took with them in death the poets that we had cherished together; and I moved further away from my youth and from the graves where my dear ones have turned to dust, the memory of Maurice de Guérin paled and grew dim. Those sublime lines—lines which I believed formulated our very destiny—quite slipped my mind:

> *Comme un fruit suspendu dans l'ombre du feuillage,*
> *Mon destin s'est formé dans l'épaisseur des bois.*
> *J'ai grandi, recouvert d'une chaleur sauvage,*
> *Et le vent qui rompait le tissu de l'ombrage*
> *Me découvrit le ciel pour la première fois.*
> *Les faveurs de nos dieux m'ont touché dès l'enfance:*
>
> *Mes plus jeunes regards ont aimé les forêts,*
> *Et mes plus jeunes pas ont suivi le silence*
> *Qui m'entraînait bien loin dans l'ombre et les secrets.*
> *Mais le jour où, du haut d'une cime perdue,*
> *Je vis (ce fut pour moi comme un brillant réveil!)*
> *Le monde parcouru par les feux du soleil,*
> *Et les champs et les eaux couchés dans l'étendue*
> *L'étendue enivra mon esprit et mes yeux;*
> *Je voulus égaler mes regards à l'espace,*
> *Et posséder sans borne en égarant ma trace,*
> *L'ouverture des champs avec celle des cieux.*

Life impoverishes us, and as we move forward in time, deprives us of our purest riches. But other men recover them for us. Just as we think we have lost everything, they restore to us a hundredfold all that our hearts had been unable to preserve. We must be deeply grateful to Father Decahors, professor at the Catholic Institute of Toulouse, whose admirable psychological biography of Maurice de Guérin helps us, without being crudely curious or vainly indiscreet, to follow the meanderings of his destiny. In the history of literature, there is only one kind of love, and it is not blind, and it does not go astray. In the case of Maurice de Guérin, there was never any erudition without feeling. To have been so fruitful, the zealous interest that led Barthès, Abel Lefranc, Ernest Zyromski, or Decahors to devote a part of their lives to Guérin must have been infused with a tender sympathy.

How surprised Maurice would have been could he have known that, a hundred years after his death, he would still be alive and young in the hearts of friends; that his cherished shade would accompany young men of twenty through the streets just as when he and Barbey d'Aurevilly crossed the Tuileries and, in the light of the setting sun, admired together the dazzling clusters of trees.

Some people will be astonished that a man can give the better part of his time to a family that has disappeared—even the de Guérin family. But Father Decahors's enormous labors helped us to measure the scope of Guérin's tragedy better than we could ever have done by ourselves. Every human passion played about this closed, melancholy adolescent who was at

once the young French Catholic and the secret wor-
shiper of Cybele; the shepherd Attis who refused to ab-
jure baptism even though it had been forced upon him;
in a word, the Guérin whom Barbey d'Aurevilly called
Endymion and who was "torn between two worlds."

A strange thing in this drama is that the most famous
figures—Lamennais, Lacordaire—play a supernumerary
role. They did not understand Maurice. These self-
styled connoisseurs of the human spirit passed by him
and scarcely turned to glance at him. Unfortunately,
while Lamennais was inflating the bellows of his
Paroles d'un croyant at La Chênaie, no one was on hand
to prophesy how, of all that was written in that somber
house, we preserve nothing except for the pages of the
Journal that Maurice de Guérin, alone in his little
room, was secretly setting down in a green notebook.

Only the most ardent love or the most patient friendship could penetrate the dense fog of self-doubt,
timidity, lassitude, and physical frailty behind which
Maurice de Guérin concealed himself, and reach his
incandescent heart. Only his sister Eugénie (and perhaps
Barbey) had to make no effort to do so, for, as Gilbert
Périer wrote of Blaise and Jacqueline Pascal, their two
hearts were one. By some trick of fate, this René's passionate yet utterly pure sister eclipsed her beloved
brother's fame after his death. Today Maurice de
Guérin has resumed his rightful place without causing
Eugénie in any sense to lose hers.

Indeed, quite the contrary has happened. We no
longer love this saintly daughter of Le Cayla only for

the humble scent of lavender and fennel that rises from the pages of the *Journal*. For she struggled with sublime faith for her brother's salvation, and suffered with him in the immense drama of a young heart that belonged first to God but, little by little, gave in to earthly enchantments and, like lightning, burned between heaven and earth. The poor country girl in her kitchen in Le Cayla seems, in human terms, much the weaker as she recites the Angelus, unaware that, at that same moment, Maurice de Guérin, handsome and elegant, is sitting at a table in the Café Anglais. Yet, in the end, Eugénie was the stronger; she lifted in her arms the brother she had carried as a child and laid his body at the feet of the God who is hidden in the little church at Andillac.

This purest of young women passed unsullied through Maurice's passions; she walked with impunity on their smouldering embers. This virgin ward of God was chosen by the Baronne de Maistre to be the confidante of her wretched love for Maurice. Her innocence remained unimpaired even when she became involved in the meanest family bickering; many tears she must have caused her sister-in-law, that charming Indian, Caroline de Gervain, whom Maurice had to pretend to love to his death. One can imagine how the mute rivalry between the jealous young woman and the older, embittered sister closed round the bed where he lay dying, and how he watched and was torn by it. Yet the two women took him back to Le Cayla together, and he died lying between their two watchful hearts. Then, two weeks after his death, Caroline went off and vanished. Eugénie remained by his grave, alone, at last, victorious as she bent over her memories, the almost savage guardian of a beloved memory that the world still strives to purloin from God.

CHARLES DU BOS

Charles Du Bos was one of the rare men for whom the life of the mind is of primary importance. All the events in his daily existence, both great and small, were of a spiritual order. Let an idea occur to him in the course of his reading: the complexion of his whole day immediately changed, his pain was eased, and the courage to refuse to die was restored to him.

If by criticism we mean judgment and classification, Du Bos could not be called a critic. He acted as critic in this sense only by making an initial distinction between the writers he found worthy of his attention and those whose existence he declined to recognize. His partiality for greatness was inflexible, and it may be that his horror of the ordinary sometimes diverted him from work of genuine merit. He never damned a book, however, and it was a waste of time to try to wring a judgment out of him. He would not reject a book; he simply took no cognizance of it.

Once Du Bos found that an author, whether living or dead, possessed the quality that he insisted was paramount, the attention he would bestow upon him would still not be a judgment. Du Bos went always to the hidden essence of a book, to the core of the destiny it reflected; he had a wonderful aptitude for reliving what he read for his own enrichment and pleasure.

Du Bos's mother was English, and his culture was confluent. He sought and found companionable peers in the cultures of England and Germany; in the literature and history of both he was deeply versed. He took only the ways that went as his own did. He moved slowly, even with excessive scruple; he was careful never to propose anything that he could not support with a quotation, was always mindful of context and chronology.

His sympathetic appreciation sometimes led him to judge friends too generously and to speak of them as if they were Goethe himself, but he combined with this a degree of intellectual probity such as my admiration has not found in any other contemporary. At one time, we were both involved in publishing a review that has since gone out of existence, and I remember his anguish when he was pressed, for reasons of orthodoxy, to make some cuts in a quotation from Coventry Patmore. Even after Du Bos's conversion, his skittish fastidiousness could conceive of transgressions other than those that are the concern of the confessional.

Because he reverenced the ideas of others and feared he might betray their thoughts, Du Bos made excessive use of quotations. While his choice has always seemed uniquely fine (as otherwise with Sainte-Beuve), their sheer quantity encumbered and obstructed his critical studies. Nor is that the least of the difficulties that he inflicted on his reader.

The reader! Charles Du Bos did not consider the reader; he concentrated all his attention on the author under review. His mind went back and forth, forth and back between himself and the writer via his own subterranean routes, without caring much if he was being followed or not; when it did indeed bother him, then he deliberately ran the risk of shutting off the outside world in order to remain closeted with the object of his study.

This gently inflexible mind yielded to no pressure but its own. Who could dare boast of ever having won the slightest concession from him? He bowed to no professional demands. In his later years, he refused even to collaborate with anyone because he preferred not to subject himself to any limitation on the full expression of his ideas. Not one among us has made less of a career than he; yet, by a strange reversal, his rigorous standards have given his friends a lofty sense of their literary vocation. I never came back from visiting Charles Du Bos, I have never reread any of the studies with which he honored my books (an admirable review of *Desert de l'amour* in the *Nouvelle Revue Française* and, especially, the profound little book in which he discusses the problem of the Catholic novelist in terms of my work) without feeling a little ashamed of anything I had published that was superficial or hasty, or without understanding more clearly than before that the act of writing is serious and grave, that it is rife with consequences, and that it engages infinitely more than the writer's own person.

As for Du Bos, he wanted nothing more than to reach a few readers among the European intellectual élite; he seemed to expect from his profound explorations among the living and the dead nothing more than the enrichment of an inner life oriented entirely toward God. I doubt that he ever lost his sense of his own worth. This fragile being who was all tremulous intelligence, who was exposed, naked and defenseless, before his harsh fellow man and hostile circumstance as well as illness; this creature so little adapted to daily reality that he never achieved stability or even security in this enemy world; this disarmed scholar who, had he not embraced Christ during the last twelve years of his life, and who if he had not had even for his body's sake the aid of the sacraments, would unquestionably have left us long before that—this man possessed a serene awareness of his own power, that power of the mind over other minds, of which Pascal spoke.

He used to allude to his "posthumes" in the tone of voice of someone who knows that the future belongs to him. The guaranteed-for-a-lifetime fame of his contemporaries impressed him less than did the perennial renascence of Stendhal, Nietzsche, and Kierkegaard. His reading, and even more, his suffering, his prayers and daily communion, and every revelation that came to him from God and man nourished his *Journal,* some fragments of which have been published; it is the *Journal,* rather than his *Approximations* that is likely to assure him the place to which he aspired: a place in the shadow of the masters, his familiars and comforters.

This short book runs into danger because of its form. Charles Du Bos talked more than he wrote. And more than anyone else I know, he talked, as the popular expression goes, "like a book." I have never heard anyone speak in better constructed or more skilfully articulated sentences, with greater flashes of brilliance or compression, than he. To this gift which enabled him to dictate directly (any other method of work would have been painful for him, anyhow, because of his illness) he owed his very special style. Wthout being at all oratorical, it is "spoken." It coils back on itself, detours, follows no apparent logic, and is entirely attuned to motions and nuances and the groping scrupulousness of a mind that senses rather than knows where it is going. Somewhere Du Bos admiringly cites Ricardo Guiraldes: *"Et mon âme marche dans la phrase comme un aveugle plein de lumière. . . ."*

There is much I could say about the kind of Christian Du Bos was, for I had forged the closest of bonds with him and in the gravest hours of my life came to know him profoundly. His conversion may be viewed as the transformation of knowledge into love. Culture does not separate great spirits from God. The example of Du Bos bears witness to the fact that the kingdom Christ said is within us is sometimes the terminus but is also the point of a new departure in the uninterrupted quest that, through the centuries, the conscious element of the human species pursues along all the inte-

rior pathways of the spirit. The search is at once cautious
and audacious, it shrinks at nothing it discovers. Charles
Du Bos followed it until he had again found the God
from whom his naturally Christian soul had never
strayed far, for even in the period when he rejected
dogma he did not stop believing in the depths of his
soul. He once wrote that there is no instance of Grace
being refused to "those who do not refuse to go as far
as their own soul."

In time his warm concern for other people became
more disinterested. No one came in contact with him
whom he did not help. With what respect and benevo-
lence he received confidences of errant human love!
What a welcome was assured any ravaged heart that
the winds of Grace guided to his door! Those who will
testify before God to this are legion.

He responded to every call for help, brushed aside no
outstretched hand. After his months of exile in
America, only the illness in which God enfolded him
more and more closely kept him from those whom he
was aiding. Although his friends refused to believe
that he was really ill, he had intimate knowledge of
the atrocious barrenness, the wasteland, of physical suffering. But death cannot be imaginary. Du Bos knew
that, some day, he would convince us. He had long
been resigned to the gulf that yawns between the
healthy and the sick. "It requires something approaching genius for a well man to understand a sick one," he
wrote, "and for a sick man always to be pleasant to the
well requires something approaching saintliness. . . ."

Death cannot be imaginary. But those who believe in their own soul suffer less from death than other men, even in the physical sense of the word. We all felt it that morning: the precious remains that we were abandoning in the little cemetery of Celle-Saint-Cloud over which the great trees, draped in mist, stand guard —this corpse was no longer Du Bos. Du Bos, we were sure, was going back to Paris with us; he had so many secrets still to tell us; he had not finished enriching our minds or, even more, preparing our hearts for a good death, a death like his own, gentle and saintly sleep, a death that is the repose of love.

II

Charles Du Bos's almost excessive courtesy was one form of his charity. The dignity he preserved in the presence of every one with whom he spoke (it variously irritated or amused us) derived, it seems to me, from his faith in his own soul and in the soul of each of us. Just as with his conversion knowledge had turned to love, so the consideration and exquisite social manner that he carried to such lengths were tokens of his respect for the human mind and of his veneration for the human soul. This attitude is manifest throughout his criticism, so unlike what all too often passes for such in the Catholic press. It deals with a book with attentive scruple because it emanates from a writer who venerates the presence of the spirit in the works of the mind.

He received sinners in the same fashion. He knew

that the guilty soul imparts some of its own greatness to the aberrations of passion. Not that he had any leniency toward sin, but he showed the men and women who confided in him how in their erring passion a sign of greatness was present and made manifest even in the wound, even in the abasement itself.

He shunned even those venial offenses that concern the confessional only indirectly or not at all: harshness, scorn, unwillingness to understand and share in another's problem, the impulse to humiliate and demean a man in his own eyes. The human qualities that are infused with Grace are what I loved in Charles Du Bos. There is probably no such thing as a pious cad; if the caddishness is authentic, then the piety can only be false. The delicacy of Du Bos toward his Christian and non-Christian friends, and especially his respect for the ideas and intentions of others, should serve as an example to all.

The criticism of Du Bos gave added stature to its subject. A book was not magnified under his scrutiny through any untoward partiality or flattery, however. The struggle between Jacob and the angel lies at the root of all great works worthy of the name, and of this he appointed himself arbiter with a subtlety that was simply scrupulousness carried to the extreme.

As he lay dying, he talked again of Nietzsche; he asked for Bach to be played. While he read and meditated on the daily office and was the most "practicing," the most devout of Christians, he never believed that the Bible had to separate him from the poets, philosophers, painters, and musicians whose testimony he tirelessly collected:

> Car c'est vraiment, Seigneur, le meilleur témoignage
> Que nous puissions donner de notre dignité
> Que cet ardent sanglot qui roule d'âge en âge. . . .

The lesson Du Bos teaches us is that intelligence is the source of love. The God of the meek, the God of the poor, is a Spirit, as the Sequence of Pentecost teaches us It is only fools who insist that God prefers fools. The head that rested on the bosom of Our Lord during the Last Supper radiated genius and already carried within it the germ of the Gospel of the Word. From Saint Paul to Saint Augustine, from Saint Bonaventure to Saint Thomas Aquinas, from Saint Francis of Assisi to Saint John of the Cross, from Saint Ignatius to Saint Francis of Sales—I glimpse among the well-beloved sons of the Father only men who were inspired. They had not only noble but lively minds. They were thinking men, and Charles Du Bos did not apologize for cherishing them for humanistic, philosophical, and artistic reasons. They helped him to approach the most profane works, sometimes those most burdened with impurities, and unmask the immortal soul concealed within.

ANNA DE NOAILLES

It is amazing to see a writer's work established in its permanent niche in literature immediately upon death. This happened in the case of Anna de Noailles. We could not have challenged the fact that she was important, but up until the very last we could have disputed the rank she would ultimately hold among French poets. Then she vanished like a mist, and the peaks of her enduring work were soaring above us. That slender mortal body had indeed concealed from us a whole world.

The miracle is all the more abrupt in the case of an artist who had mingled with society, submitted to its rituals, been a friend whom one familiarly called Marcel and found an agreeable, complex, gossipy man; or had been a woman called Anna who was always late and who, when invited to dine, kept everyone from sitting down at table until nine-thirty. These people die, and promptly *La recherche du temps perdu* of Marcel Proust and the poetry of the Comtesse de Noailles are assigned to the place in world literature that they will never lose.

"The living are not venerable." I think it was Mme. de Noailles herself who wrote that. They are the less venerable if they belong to a coterie, if they more or less abide by its conventions and, to the extent that they evade them, irritate or amuse the members of their small world who suppose themselves their peers. Such equality seems a fact in social terms, until from the bier bearing the motionless creature whose sallies had made us laugh only the evening before, a star rises to take its place in the constellation of our most cherished poets.

After such a transfiguration, how discomfiting it is

when the poet's correspondence is published. It seems incredible that the letters of Proust and *Du côté de chez Swann* could have been written by the same man. Was the master of such fearsomely rigorous analysis also this too amiable friend dabbling in petty squabbles and complications, this ludicrous flatterer flaunting his insufferable false humility, this gossip who contributed to the hyperboles of fashionable chit-chat?

It appears that, toward the end of his life, Proust had a presentiment of the greatness death was to assure him. The dying Caesar spoke mockingly when he said, "I feel I am becoming a god." But the silence and solitude that Marcel Proust created about his bed during the last two years of his life, his insistence that even his closest friends stay away, and his almost ferocious detachment testify to his feeling that he was becoming literally immortal. In a similar way, Mme. de Noailles never allowed the faintest trace of her prodigious wordly wit to appear in her poetry. She refused to let the lesser part of her mind collaborate even slightly in work that should survive so long as human memory endures.

This cleavage between the lives and work of the great writers of society seems much less clear-cut in the case of the *poètes maudits*. These men may be exempt from all the rules, but at the same time they are slaves to the suffering of the outcast in a society that has no place for him.

The censure that the world heaped on Baudelaire and Verlaine, the prayers and curses on *Les fleurs du mal* and *Sagesse,* reflect this. It is impossible to separate the frightful personal fate of these men from the immortal cries of pain wrenched from them. The suffering of an Anna de Noailles or of a Marcel Proust is no less real. But despite illness and anguish, the luxurious, sheltered life and the atmosphere of adulation that surrounded Mme. de Noailles especially seem to have no direct connection with poetry of despair. The despair here is of a metaphysical nature, expressed in the monotonous, sublime clamorings of a creature who has been overwhelmed, who held the universe in her arms and whom it had profited nothing to have gained the universe.

The genius of Baudelaire, Verlaine, and Rimbaud was nourished by their everyday lives. If I may put it so, their work is rooted in the earth, in mud. In his fascinating book, *Verlaine tel qu'il fut,* M. François Porché tells us nothing, literally and absolutely nothing, that is not implicit in each line of *La bonne chanson, Sagesse, Parallèlement,* and *Amour.* Verlaine's verse is wedded to the rhythm of his dreadful life. On the other hand, Mme. de Noailles could write *L'histoire de ma vie* without its being the story of her poetry. Obviously I am not speaking here of the hidden dramas of the mind and heart.

The "bemired grandeur," the "sublime ignominy" of Verlaine fertilized his verse. The enchanting poems of *Sagesse* could rise toward Christ and His Mother *"comme la guêpe vole au lis épanoui"* only from the cell where Paul Verlaine, tried and condemned by common law, touched the depths of humiliation and shame. He paid for every one of his great works in blood, tears, and his honor as a man. His pathetic personal story still scandalizes his biographers; they have never left off thanking God that He did not make them like that "swine," nor will they ever leave off, for the sad tale must be told so long as his beloved voice has not fallen silent. His immortal work immortalizes his drunkenness, alas, and his fearsome way of life.

Because the poetry of Baudelaire and Verlaine echoes their personal anguish, it makes their lives unforgettable. One could say of other writers, among them some of the greatest, that their own survival—the survival of their personality, that is—makes their works endure. Chateaubriand interests us more than Chateaubriand's books. Of all the volumes he produced, we respond to the *Mémoires d'outre-tombe* because this book shows us the whole man (often without his knowing it). His others interest us chiefly insofar as they help us to know him better. It is the same with Rousseau. Almost everything he wrote seems hard to read today except for the *Confessions* and the *Rêveries,* where again the whole man is to be found. We are still too close to Barrès and his books are still too controversial for us to think of ranking him among such writers as these. (For that matter, nothing is more arbitrary than such classifications, but it is generally conceded that Barrès's work is a landmark in the history of French literature.) The younger generation, it appears, misunderstands or is indifferent to his best writing but is curious to know what kind of man he was. And much as we loved him, much as we have cherished his books, from *Sous l'oeil des Barbares* to *Jardin sur l'Oronte,* we, too, have looked for the man, for the secret of his particular attitude toward the world, his way of submitting to the finishing processes of life. It was Barrès himself whom we pursued from book to book.

We still continue to look in what he wrote primarily for the commentary on a personal destiny that was replete with grandeur. With passionate eagerness, we open each volume of the posthumous "Cahiers"— the memories from beyond the grave that he had no time to retouch—in which all that his stormy soul concealed in its depths, all that shunned exposure, gushes to the surface and surrenders to us. An unpublished fragment appearing not long ago in the *Revue universelle* contained, in addition to an admirable meditation on religion, admissions that are astonishing from a man who could be so scathingly contemptuous; they hold a secret sweetness, strike a tender broken note such as we had not heard since the closing pages of *Sous l'oeil des Barbares.* Here it sounds again, speaking directly to our hearts:

"There are days when one is all love, incapable of sleep, stirred by the star-filled sky, the silence, the resigned memory of the dead, the flight of time, the overflowing of the heart, isolation. . . ."

II

Too much happiness is a dangerous thing. The ancients were right to fear too consistent good luck; in the end, fortune's favorite is almost always destroyed.

Happiness pursues some people as relentlessly as if it were unhappiness, and this spells misfortune indeed. When I first saw Anna de Noailles, she was in the full splendor of her youthful glory. Other women were beautiful, but only she possessed the beauty that is transfigured by genius. She was born a princess; on the day of her marriage, she received one of the greatest and most glorious names of France; she had no sooner assumed it than the brightness of her own genius cast the shining annals of this famous family into the shadows. Henceforth, the name de Noailles will no longer call to mind the conqueror of Cérisoles, or the Archbishop of Paris who secretly befriended the Jansenist and for whom Racine wrote the history of Port Royal, or three Marshals of France—but this young Minerva, weaned from all prudence, responsive only to her own intoxication, who, like Goethe's Euphorion, cast herself headlong *"dans un espace plein de douleur. . . ."*

How fortunate this woman was in her despair! Every moment of her life she rejoiced in the full possession of her genius, whether as poet she submitted in private to her sublime inspiration or whether she was reigning over the salons of Paris like a queen.

Those were the glorious days. The instant she appeared we would crowd around her. She was in a perpetual swoon, yet somehow her very exhaustion fed and sustained her intoxication. She could make her young admirers laugh to the point of tears, as her poems made them drunk on melancholy in their lonely rooms at night. She was quick to detect the absurd in others with what Saint-Simon called "murderous precision," and she would pounce on her victims like a furious, joyous bee. She was quite heedless of the sting she left imbedded, audaciously oblivious that a humiliated vanity nurses its painful memories. Like Marie Antoinette, that other young and idolized queen, she wounded more hearts than she charmed.

So long as we lack some one thing, we still hope to achieve it, and we therefore cannot know despair. But the royal mentor of our youth lacked nothing and therefore could achieve the despair that is so necessary to poets, and that came to her as a kind of bonus. One must have everything to value nothing, possess all in order to have the right to despise all. No detachment is possible without possession, for how can we separate ourselves from what we do not have?

This human goddess toward whom fate was so treacherously prodigal knew no humble wish, no "lack" that could divert her from thinking of death. No routine concern deflected her from her single misfortune (the only one that no power on heaven or earth could spare her) of having been born mortal and of giving her heart only to creatures as ephemeral as she herself. The evanescence, the dissolution, and the flight of

the beloved became the essential motif of her poetry
in which she celebrated the gardens of this world and
a firmament purely human. The Bergsonian theme of
duration (which Proust was to transpose into fiction)
supplied her with a sublime source of inspiration.

But it did so until that day when it became apparent
that time would also alter the one possession she would
have believed unalterable—her fame. Nothing in her
long, tumultuous ascendancy could prepare her for
the inevitable trial that no one—and, especially in
France, no poet—is spared. (It was his politics, not his
poetry, that made the aging Hugo the idol of France.)

"This great torment, old age . . ." Michelin observed,
in his own declining years. He could as well have said:
this endless mounting torment of sensing from far off
the slow approach of age. It is indeed the most excru-
ciating of all torments for those whose path does not
rise in glory toward God. To endure it uncomplain-
ingly calls for intelligence and manly courage. But this
once all-conquering creature was called upon to perform the act of faith in her own genius when she was
already living among the shadows, and she responded
like a stunned, pitifully anxious woman.

We must realize that a poet's pride is only a façade.
Even among the greatest, there is not one who does
not doubt himself, who is not upset by the smallest
criticism, who does not need admiration and praise as
he needs bread and water. But we had been so confident that Mme. de Noaille's work would outlast time
that it irritated us to see her so reduced. After all, what

more had she to do than to reread *Les vivants et les morts* to be able to make allowances for the indifference of the young postwar barbarians?

This was the period when, after a long incubation, the virus of Rimbaud was beginning to show up in French poetry. As one young insolent said, in front of me, to Mme. de Noailles, "One no longer writes verse, Madame." It was the period when a poet in the lineage of Stephen Mallarmé had appeared, who was attentive to the value and weight of every word and who was the enemy of all facility. I can still see myself, shortly after the Armistice, standing in the Floury bookshop as I read Paul Valéry's *La jeune Parque* from beginning to end without pause. Thanks to Léautaud's anthology, I had known his name for years. *"Recherches volontaires, accomplissement des pensées, consentiment de l'âme à des gênes exquises, et le triomphe perpetuel du sacrifice. . . ."* Such was his own art, the opposite pole of *Coeur innombrable* and *Eblouissements*. We used to meet almost every evening at a friend's house to listen to this master of poetic perfection and purity.

But in the Muses' house are many mansions, and in those days I was still close enough to a youth that had fairly buzzed with all the poets, so that new gods did not usurp my old allegiances. Indeed, not one among us failed to remain faithful to the woman who had given voice to the passions of our youth. Perhaps we should have told her this once more, but we never dreamed that our immortal poet had need of reassurance.

Happy are they who do not fear indifference, who even look forward with anxious anticipation to the silence with which the world surrounds a declining destiny. It is best for us to leave the world before the world leaves us. One by one, the hawsers drop from the ship as it lies in drydock, but for a moment it remains motionless: although nothing holds it back, it does not begin to slide. Blessed be old age that detaches us from the world long in advance, so that the voyage into eternity can be made without a wrench. Because the world hates age, it renounces us whether or not we have the strength to renounce it. If only we had been able to show this frivolous heart our gratitude by forcing her to stand alone before her Creator. "As one grows old," René Bazin observed on the eve of his death, "as one grows old, everything goes away, but God comes."

God does come, but His approach is different for each man. Perhaps (I have always believed this) He does not treat poets like other men. Everything happens as if poets had a special mission, as if they had to give an example that only they can give, as if their life, whatever it may be, was willed to be as it is. All of them, whether they have believed in eternal life, or, like Anna de Noailles, denied it, attest to the grandeur of the human soul and to its divine calling. The poets have always protected me against doubt; even when mud-bespattered, like Rimbaud and Verlaine, they arouse my sense of an Eden-like purity, a lost purity that we must find again through humiliation and tears. Battered by every gale, drenched by spindrift, they are indeed the "lighthouses" Baudelaire called them, motionless on their rock. Apparently unable to save themselves, they burn in the darkness and our path is drowned in their light.

These inspired, revered poets may seem remote from each other, but they maintain a kind of kinship, a mysterious resemblance. The terrible vagabonds, Verlaine, Rimbaud, and the Comtesse de Noailles, born Princess of Brancovan, have a mutual vocation of ardor, suffering, and humiliated greatness. The sordid room in which Verlaine died, naked, prone on the floor, I confound in my mind with the cheap furnished room on the Rue Hamelin, where I saw Marcel Proust lie dead, and with the room on the Rue Scheffer, where the "many-chambered heart" of Anna de Noailles came to the end of its agony.

III

This illustrious woman lent her voice to our tormented youth. Her poetry was the cry of our adolescence. From others we sought comfort and light or we asked to be cradled and rocked to sleep. But it was she who attracted the passions that do not wish to be healed. What a temptation for the young heart to discover gratification—and God beyond

Admired, adored, endowed, almost encumbered, with every human talent, she was our elder by ten years and so could warn us that to possess everything is to have nothing, that it profits us nought to gain the whole world. Yet she had captured the whole world in poems in which Venice, Sorrento, and Sicily seemed more warm, more fragrant than any reality. From all the gardens of the world she gathered only those herbs required to brew the philter that Iseult shares with Tristan, and this she made us drink.

She never distinguished between love and death. Her demands went far beyond the limits of human love. In the wonderful opening poems of *Les vivants et les morts,* she could make us sense how the beloved creature takes flight even as she is held close in our arms:

> *Quelque chose de toi sans cesse m'abandonne,*
> *Car rien qu'en vivant, tu t'en vas. . . .*

She was the first to persuade us of love's deception, showing us how the beloved slips away, dissolves, betrays in perfect fidelity. Our twentieth year owes her its recognition of the disproportion between what the heart desires and what it pursues to the brink of bankruptcy. How did it serve our youthful love to attain its object, since it embraced only the form? Beauty finally apprehended bore no resemblance to what had fled from us:

> *Je me tairai, je veux, les yeux larges ouverts,*
> *Regarder quel éclat a votre vrai visage,*
> *Et si vous ressemblez à ce que j'ai souffert. . . .*

This lack of correspondence between love and the love object awakened in us a pain that was to become love itself, or, at least, all that we were given to know beyond the sensual. Human love became self-aware only through pain, so that if we did not cause pain to another, we did not know that we were loved. Lovers know each other only through the suffering they inflict, the wounds they exchange. All the anguish of our attachment to other creatures is expressed in this imperishable verse:

La paix qui m'envahit quand c'est vous qui souffrez. . . .

And yet, because both bodies are alive, even as they seek each other, nothing stops their perpetual disintegration. The poet tries in vain to fix her joy in time and place:

La terrasse est comme un navire
Qu'il fait chaud sur la mer, ce soir! . . .

Nothing is still; every parapet becomes a prow, all Nature drifts, like Tristan's ship bearing the fugitive pair toward death.

From her youth this lovely genius had looked death in the face. Like the great romantics, she never turned her eyes from it. And that is what makes her own death so astonishing. For most men, dying is an accident; they stumble and vanish through the trap door like so many unwary animals. But this woman who contemplated and, if I dare say it, held vigil by her future corpse—her silence and immobility baffle the mind. I repeat over and over to her sleeping figure Christ's words at

the Last Supper as he questions the disciples: "Do ye
now believe?" She knows now. She knows. She sees.

Is it possible that she spent a lifetime contemplating
death in vain? We have known no more avid mind, yet
death revealed to her nothing of all that lies concealed
behind its shadows. From childhood Mme. de Noailles
leaned over the abyss of eternal light, yet gave her heart
and consent to the night.

Why did we sense that, failing some unforeseeable
miracle, it had to be so? She herself seemed terribly
sure that she would never succumb to the temptation
of God, as if she had been drawn up on the bank far
from the current of Grace in which her young brethren
were swept along. She paraphrased Pascal in the sublime *Elévations* in vain; in vain she proffered God the
holocaust of her poems *("Mon Dieu, je ne sais rien, mais
je sais que je souffre . . .").* The smoke of her sacrifice
was deflected and floated earthward.

It is of no use for us to call upon God if we do not
listen. Silent attentiveness is an aspect of prayer that is
too much neglected. Her many-chambered, echoing
heart was never silent. What could this swarming bee
hear above its own admirable humming?

"Above all, one must thirst." Mme. de Noailles wrote
these words of Catherine of Siena in the margin of
"Poème de l'amour." (We all had the unfortunate habit
of appropriating the saints' noblest words and twisting
them to the purposes of our own passion!) These words
might have brought her some enlightenment, had she
understood them: "Thirst for the silence in which God

speaks." Perhaps then she would have heard the inner word addressed to Catherine of Siena: "Thou art she who is not. . . ."

That was the key to the puzzle, and Mme. de Noailles did not find it. She remained incurable, she was blinded by her own light. The human planets circling about her were visible to her only in the aura of her own radiance.

Youth slipped away; new generations burned their incense before other idols; the prostrate woman saw the dreadful ax fall on those whom she most cherished. Solitude and silence took forcible possession of her tumultuous life until, crucified by illness, she was permanently immobilized. Let us go no further; let us kneel before the mystery of those last days when, stripped of all her arms, vanquished at last, this great prophetess received perhaps the only revelations unknown to her—those that, as Pascal teaches us, are attained through humiliation alone.

BARRÈS AND CATHOLICISM

Maurice Barrès's *Cahiers,* which are full of notes and drafts for such of his books as *La grande pitié des églises de France,* are all the more tedious to me, since I haven't the slightest impulse to reread the books themselves. I skip about impatiently among all the unfinished capitals and shafts and débris of his production, which was of great intrinsic interest, in order to find the author who as a man is more absorbing today than ever. He belonged to the species of liana mind that must have a support. But he slips sometimes; he abandons the cemetery cross he had entwined himself about and climbs at random. In the *Cahiers* this is the moment to surprise him—a limited man, perhaps, but one of great penetration with brilliant flashes of intuition.

An earlier volume of the *Cahiers* revealed a profound metaphysical unease such as Barrès scarcely betrayed in his writing or in conversation. The later, on the other hand, shows him as I knew him, basing his defense of Catholicism on various considerations that had no relation to Christ's essential meaning when He said, "I am the Truth." This is understandable; Barrès was intent on answering objections from Radical Socialist deputies. Oddly, though, one feels that he was put out and even incensed when an opponent chaffingly protested, "Well now, Monsieur Barrès, do you believe all this yourself?"

I may scandalize believer and non-believer alike, but I have to confess that a man who defends Christianity without believing in it is beyond my understanding. This, so far as I can see, is accounted for only by a failure of imagination. He sees the noble and illustrious façade that the Church has erected before the world; he admires the bark of Peter steadfast above the floods of time. But he forgets the foundations. He forgets the many lives that have been offered up voluntarily and those that have been sacrificed. From generation to generation, throughout nineteen hundred years, the better part of mankind has mounted the cross of its own deliberate choice, and no amount of scorn and derision has been able to force it to climb down.

For my own part, I would make short shrift of cathedrals, liturgy, Gregorian chant, if all these things served only to glorify a little piece of unleavened bread. All the Christian virtues, the sensitive Christian conscience, the miracles of mystical love—in a word, holiness—would hold no prestige in my eyes had they been born of and rested on a lie.

Perhaps Barrès persuaded himself that convents and parsonages (to mention only ecclesiastics and monks) are inhabited exclusively by serene, joyous souls bathed in the consolations of their faith. No doubt there are many such. But even they rejoice in a peace that is not the peace the world offers. Their joy is the fruit of a continual victory over nature. It is a victory won at the price of a renunciation to which one does not submit once and for all but that one must renew every moment, in things small as well as large. This is the "little path" that led Thérèse of the Child Jesus, the martyr of Lisieux, so far and to such lofty heights.

And there are the others—the faithful who get halfway up the hill, struggle, fall, pick themselves up, give in once more, and rise again to stumble along a road that is stained with the blood of those who went before. All of them, sinners and saints, believed and trusted in one solemn assurance: "Heaven and earth will pass away, but My words will not pass away." Each and every one, saint and sinner alike, cried out in their moments of doubt or agony, "Toward whom should we turn, Lord? Thou speakest the words of eternal life!" They would scoff at merely imitating the dead. What do they care about the dust of people they have not loved? For them it is not a question of subscribing to a national tradition or of pretending to believe fables that help foster certain useful virtues. Suppose, by some impossible chance, it was revealed to them that Christ is not the Son of God; in such a case, they would no longer follow Him even for the sake of a given civilization or culture. They follow Him because He said, "I am the Christ," and they have taken Him at His word.

Some people will protest that I am wrong even to raise the question. Barrès was a non-believer, but he never supposed that those who do believe are dupes since the essential thing is, after all, to have faith. Faith, in their view, is a reality even if its object is an illusion. An illusory happiness is none the less happiness, they say; hope without a foundation is still hope; if eternity did not exist, Christians would never know it, for nothingness confounds no one.

This point of view appalls me. In any event, it could have meaning only for the pious breed that have nothing to renounce or that give up long after the world has given them up—the ones who bring to God the leavings of self that no one else wants. Yes, this type is sure to win the wager Pascal offers. But what about the others? The young people consecrated to God in all the vigor and sensitivity of their youth? After all, they have renounced something real. Our human happiness, miserable as it may be, is, after all, real. Love seems precarious or absurd to us simply because we know it is only a caricature of union with the divine. Yet if such union were only a snare, if the promise of eternal life had never reverberated throughout the world, then this wretched human love would have been a priceless pearl, precious above all other things, and man would have been compelled to sell all he possessed, renounce all, to win it.

But *the Word became flesh.* The Cross thus became worthy of worship but only because He was nailed to it. Without the Word, the Cross would be a gallows—nothing more.

Let me say again, I realize that Barrès wished to achieve something practical and concrete for the well-being of the Church in France; I know that he was not offering personal motives for his own attachment to Christianity, and that he was searching for reasons calculated to convince men bereft of all belief, like Jaurès, Briand, and Sembat. But let us concede that these men were not bereft of good sense when they asked Barrès the question no defender of the Church has the right to evade (whether he fights from before the altar or outside in the church square): "What is *your* opinion of Christ?"

GEORGES DUHAMEL

In some men love for music and poetry is a defense against life. Because they are born without a protective shell, they try to move through life surrounded by a cloud of harmony, much as certain fish stir up the water around them to escape being devoured by their fellows. In this sense, Bach and Mozart protect Duhamel. Not that he bears any resemblance to etherealized spirits who believe that the poetic is the antithesis of the real. I read recently how a friend of mine used to shock his young wife by asking her, when he came home after a day's work, the simple, childish, human question: "What's for dinner this evening?"

For Duhamel, bread and wine—especially wine—and countless cheeses and all that Nature heaps on the table of her well-loved children are very real. He is profoundly attached to life, but for all that he is constantly shattered by it. He is neither the "pacifist" nor the "humanitarian" he was believed to be. In the spiritual sense, the author of *Civilisation* is a great war casualty: he is a man who has never recovered from what he saw every day for four years.

Many actors in the same conflict preserved only an abstract awareness of their experience. What a tremendous privilege in wartime to be a medical officer, for whom the physical world is real and paramount! But the essential gift of the man who wrote *Vie des mar-*

tyres is imagination of the heart; he had the ability to share the suffering of others, to relive it in himself.

Duhamel was human—all too human; he would never have been able to endure the agony of others' pain without some appropriate defense—in his case, his memory of music. Even today, when no man's pitiful life blood is spilling over his hands, it protects him, for everyday life is quite enough to bathe one in others' blood.

Duhamel has always found the melody he himself needed for shelter. And if a friend could not remember a particular air that was dear to him, Duhamel reached down within himself and, little by little, drew it up from that mysterious lair where all the music of the world seemed to lie enchained.

He did not always fetch it up on the instant. For hours and hours, Orpheus may have wandered in the limbo of sleeping sound—Duhamel went on laughing and talking. Nothing suggested that a part of him was working secretly to discover the charm that will awaken the elusive phrase.

I remember one summer at Estoril when I heard his friendly voice at the other end of the wire: "I've found your rondo!" It was a Mozart rondo I had been talking about to him the evening before; we had tried to remember it, but neither of us could. As I was hurrying down to rejoin the friend who had rescued my melody from silence, suddenly the tune came back to me too, like a child delivered.

For this parent of Salavin and the Pasquier, inspiration was born of his passionate and bitter knowledge of men, a knowledge that was hardly come by but that acts as his shield against the world's hostility. The greatest creative people draw from brute reality some essential thing that protects and saves them. We would be surprised to know the exact and ridiculous misery that lies at the source of this or that concerto by Beethoven or even the swallow-songs of Mozart.

I remember one summer day, in the living room at Valmondois, a young girl was sitting at the piano and Duhamel was leaning over it; note by note he was breathing an andante that emerged hesitatingly at first, then burst forth like a spring freed from ice.

I also remember the scene of our setting out on the Tagus; the wife of my friend, sitting in the prow of the boat, was softly reciting the sublime poem Verlaine had inspired in Claudel. From the bowels of the ship, the young Portuguese girls came up, one by one, drawn by Blanche Albane's voice. In the same way, Duhamel, from the depths of a memory gorged on music, was able to discover and to express sweet melodies.

RENAN AND SALVATION

When I first used to think about Renan, whose inner debate was to become the drama of a whole era, I never imagined a young man as poor as he was obscure. I received my first (and most deserved) slaps from Paul Souday, in 1910, via *le Temps,* for having written in reply to some inquiry, "What a bore that hypocrite Renan is!" Twenty years were to pass by before I discovered that every word in Renan's private papers speaks of feelings I have experienced, torments I have known, temptations against which I have had to struggle.

For the Christian, Renan's drama is that of a man whose love of truth separates him from the truth. Base motives never drove him from God. The Christian virtues never weighed heavily on him, and almost to the end of his life he was modest to the point of frugality. In his heart, a heart that was never closed to God, he accepted the asceticism and mystique of the Catholic Church. In his heart he perceived, heard, and embraced the Lord whom he renounced for reasons of philology. He had the misfortune to base his hope in the love that renews both the face of the earth and the heart of man on two exegetical questions: the Messianic interpretation of a psalm and the authorship of the Pentateuch.

Renan did not actually deny that divine love exists. Like a good Hegelian, he established his position in terms of contradiction. If, as he was convinced, science demonstrates that the impression made on him by a Being whom he has adored and whose name alone still makes him tremble, is utterly meaningless and in no way disproves the reality of nothingness, he did not try to erase its stamp. He left everything up in the air, and he taught his daughter, "It is impossible not to believe in immortality, you know. Believe in it, and don't listen to anyone else, even if they quote me to you."

We know that, from the Christian point of view, the lust of the mind is as fearful as the lust of the flesh. A stream of mortal lava flows from Renan. But I feel awfully far away from the simplicities of my youth, when I could damn a man as lightheartedly as one of Claudel's poems proposes. The mystery of the judgments of God on each of us as individuals is the mystery of mercy itself. The Christian is not forbidden to try to imagine through which fault mercy will seep into a man's destiny; and I, on my part, imagine that in Renan's case it was his devotion to what he believed was the truth, (just as in that of Gide it would be total sincerity, love for the underprivileged, and detachment).

Some one once said, in the course of a casual conversation, that after all we don't know what God thought of Protestants. One of the people present, who was most devout, broke in to say, "Well, I know!" which made the first speaker smile. But then, as he thought about it, he realized that he and almost all Christians, no matter to which of the various sects they belong, share this attitude, although they might not always show it so frankly.

But, actually, we do not know. The theologian has a perfect right to insist that he knows how God judges a heresy but not how He judges the heretic. I have known people who, as they lay dying, steeled themselves to reject the summons of a bliss to which they could have responded deeply but from which their minds withheld assent. Did they say no from scruple? Or from pride, or obstinacy? If it was from scruple, perhaps God loved them still.

"Truth to whatever extreme! Truth at any price!" young Renan cried in the seminary and he was still affirming it as the famous old man whose views so impressed those of the same turn of mind as Lemaître and Anatole France. The image, however, of the man—torn and divided against himself as he was for more than half a century—contradicts these effusions. The smile of the sprightly old skeptic belies his child's soul where God still reigns, and his student's heart that is indelibly marked with the name of Jesus.

"Truth to whatever extreme!" What an admission! The truth cannot be strained or pushed to extremes, but the speculations of historical criticism can be. "Truth at any price?" Yes, even at the price of truth.

And now let us listen attentively to his ceaseless cry as he lay dying: "Have pity on me!" He had once said, "I will pray when I am dying. We pray all the time without realizing it." And he kept repeating, "Have pity on me!" Perhaps in the mind of God a little boy of six, Ernest Psichari, had already been chosen to atone for the wrong that his grandfather had done. Yes, surely so, but the boy was also chosen to bear witness as a visible sign of the Father's compassion for those who seek Him. The God Renan renounced did not deny him but remained with him and with all his people who had received God's blessing.

SHAKESPEARE ON HISTORY

In *Illusions perdues,* Balzac admiringly cites the saying, "Collective crimes implicate no one." But what crime is not collective? Even if the murderer confronts his victim alone, his accomplices among the living and the dead could readily be found. Yet only he is tried, only he pays the penalty.

History treats collective crimes the way Society treats individual murders; it requires only a few names and faces. It has charged Charles IX and Catherine de Medici with the crushing responsibility for the Saint Bartholomew's Day Massacre, a collective crime if ever there was one. A few Montagnards share with Robespierre the odium of the Terror and the decrees passed by the National Convention.

Our European war leaders are well aware of this pattern. Peace is barely restored before they publish their memoirs and, armed to the teeth, busily defend themselves and attack their fellow-professionals with a vengeance. Fear of History's verdict has inspired more books than you could count. A statesman or military leader may be most firmly persuaded of his own innocence but he is no less apprehensive, and he is right. History is not impartial. Qualified witnesses, pro and con, succeed each other century after century; they besiege the bar of History, lustily exchanging blow for blow, for men's passions survive the scourge of violence they precipitate.

Curiously enough, when it occurs to a playwright (if he is called Shakespeare) to put historical characters on the stage, and if he permits his own ideas and inventiveness to control the situation, he offends Justice less than does official history. I was struck by this recently as I was rereading, one after another, Shakespeare's Histories (all the *Henrys, Richard II and III, King John*). I had found them tedious before and had never really gotten into them, but the drama of war that we ourselves have come through has strangely illuminated the beauty of these plays.

Shakespeare shows us that the source of all history lies in human emotions. The destiny of England has been guided by passions that he reveals to us in these plays; it has been incarnate in a few beings who belonged to the breed whose fearful secret Napoleon once let slip: "What do a million lives mean to me?"

Shakespeare has helped me follow with my mind's eye the leading roles played in our wars, and a few magazines have helped, too, I must admit. I remember, for example, a photo in which Stalin, standing behind the very correct German diplomats, looked as if he had blood-smeared jaws, and another, taken in Poland, which showed Chancellor Hitler and his Minister of Foreign Affairs walking along a gravelly roadbed, slightly stooped, their hands clasped behind their backs, and their feet seeming to be dragging an invisible ball and chain.

Shakespeare knew what the Reichschancellor said to himself when he was alone and leaned his forehead against the windowpane, or when he looked at himself in a mirror, or touched his cheek, murmuring, "This is I, Hitler. . . ." Or when the vision of a gutted Warsaw froze him motionless in the middle of the room. Perhaps, like Richard III in the horror of his last night, he murmured:

> What do I fear? Myself? There's none else by:
> Richard loves Richard; that is, I am I. . . .

The restlessly darting thoughts of the master of Germany, his agonies, and his suspicions—Shakespeare knew them all, as he knew all the conflicts of interest, all the stirrings of jealousy, the bitterness and fear enveloping the malefic man who, on September 1, 1939, gave the signal summoning death.

Like our human courts, like posterity, Shakespeare denounces the guilty person, the responsible individual. But by a miracle of genius he shows him to us encircled and engulfed by necessity; Shakespeare does not separate the man from the obscure forces that conjoined to culminate in a particular nature brimming with insolent guilt. In this fashion, Art prevails over History when it judges the creatures of History. To the end Shakespeare's vilest assassin preserves the excuse that at every moment of his life he is a human being caught up in a maelstrom of events that are not determined by him. His thirst to dominate does not spring from his own life; it comes from further away.

Above these fleeting human destinies that to us seem so bloody shine the great constellations, indifferent to human criminal passion. The same moonlight that during these last evenings I have watched sleeping in the mists that enfold the now stripped vineyards makes me, in Shakespeare's theater, aware of the harmony that reigns over a world whose silence is undisturbed by struggles we think of as titanic.

It is at this point that Shakespeare becomes dangerous reading for us in these times that we must live through, when he whispers to us through the lips of the dying Cleopatra:

> All's but naught;
> Patience is sottish, and impatience does
> Become a dog that's mad.

Unlike our own Racine, Shakespeare does not hold us captive to a humanity that is lucid even though blind to all outside itself. (If Phèdre prays to the sun, it is because she is its carnal descendant.) Shakespeare is not imprisoned by tragedy limited to the human dimension. He leads us out onto the heath where I imagine

> What time the shepherd, blowing of his nails,
> Can neither call it perfect day nor night.

He forces us to remove ourselves from the game, to stand off, to rise above our indignation and our hate, above all the emotions a man must keep alive in his heart during a war; he tears from us the cry of Edward of York in *Henry VI*:

For never henceforth shall I joy again,
Never, O never, shall I see more joy!

More than one intellectual earnestly laboring to keep his mind in step is unconsciously exposed to this kind of abdication. And without question, one of the stakes we have in these times is each man's right to think as he thinks, if I may put it so. None the less, we must not allow ourselves to escape through the inner door to which Shakespeare holds the key. It opens on a void.

MARCEL PROUST

An author's chances to survive cannot be easily estimated by his contemporaries. In very few cases can we be sure that such and such a work will endure. But some do take their permanent place in literature before our eyes, never to leave it. The worst that can befall them is that they may go out of style. The fact that an early admirer of Proust becomes disaffected proves nothing against *A la recherche du temps perdu*. It simply means that, for whatever meager reasons he adduces for his disenchantment, a critic puts *himself* where *he* belongs.

Once our first bedazzlement had passed, we quickly learned Proust's limitations, particularly his inability to center the successive states of consciousness of his heroes; that is, to sense what constituted the individual core of each. We know now what not to ask of him.

But the most absurd reproach to aim at him is that he is indifferent to social problems.

Proust's contribution in this area is of inestimable value precisely because he studied the world without any of the preoccupations that so seriously encumber the work of, say, Bourget. The most effective revolutionaries among writers are not those who champion this or that system but those who deepen our knowledge of man as he really is, who make us attentive to the undercurrents created in a human being by the conflict between social pressures and his own passions and vices.

It was not Proust's vocation to teach us the Gospel according to Taine, or according to Sorel, or according to Marx. He belonged to that small group of writers who, in every generation, "by decree of the supreme powers," are granted a brief, fleeting moment in which to correct the human balance.

Each makes use of his particular talents. Bourget was essentially an observer who defined the ills of society, traced their causes, and did not hesitate to prescribe the cures. No one could claim that Proust ever saw things in this sense. It is not in terms of observation but of absorption that he is to be discussed. Throughout a seemingly futile youth he absorbed everything; he incorporated, he made part of himself, a world that he subsequently rediscovered within himself in what is one of the greatest poetic miracles of our literature. What he recreated for us is not a complete universe, of course, but it is authentic, enduring, and fluid. It would never

have occurred to him to describe something he knew
only from the outside, something that was not consub-
stantial with him. A work like Jules Romain's *Les
hommes de bonne volonté*—or at least certain chapters
in it—help us to understand the error that Proust was
most careful not to commit.

Herein lies the social importance of Proust's writing.
No one would deny it today were it not that knowledge
of man and of his true condition is the last concern of
the reformers and revolutionaries of whatever stamp
who urge their nostrums on us. Let me make myself
clear: Proust did not produce a revolutionary work
because he described a corrupt society, for societies
seen through the eyes of a psychologist or moralist
always seem rotten. (If a Russian Proust existed, what
a hell he would paint for us!) But Proust led us farther
than any of his predecessors into that secret world over
which the lawmaker has no power. He laid bare all the
infection that suppurates under the iron chains of
tyranny as well as beneath the harness of custom and
the trappings of propriety. What consequences can be
drawn from such a terrible demonstration! But the
people who could profit from his lesson don't read him,
and now the snobs are withdrawing too, leaving Proust
with his real friends, a small group that will not change.
If it is possible—and I believe it is—to determine the
chances of survival for a given work by taking into
account both its veracity and its power of poetic sug-
gestion, then *A la recherche du temps perdu* is the sole
contemporary work whose survival cannot be doubted.

D. H. LAWRENCE

The tremendous buzzing above my head is not bees in swarm but the humming of the cockchafers. They light on the young leaves, which are not yet strong enough to hold them, and down they tumble on the page where I have been writing what He says to Her and what She says to Him. Even if I lean back and look up, I can't see any birds through the foliage, but they seem to have gotten quite drunk on their own warbling. I recognize the song of the nightingale. And if Delamain were here, he could tell me the name of the one that repeats over and over its tender, beguiling lament.

The sun is gently healing the April frostbite, and the buds are beginning to swell on the vines. There may be some wine, after all. I see the nightingale now! I feel something near to pity for that swollen, throbbing throat—a true Malibran! But last evening the crickets in the vineyard drowned it out. Every single invisible cricket vibrates with a savage frenzy; if I lean my ear close to them, my eardrum hurts.

That plump gray cuckoo fluttering about in the arbor will not sing for fear I'll notice him. The spring will not let me read. The last of the lilacs and the first hawthorns spill such fragrance through the air that my book slips from my hands. And yet it was speaking to me about D. H. Lawrence. Lawrence and Katherine Mansfield are still my best English friends. I can only understand and like the English after they are dead; it takes a thousand critics, a thousand published letters, private journals, the inside information furnished by M. Maurois, and a few good translations to persuade me that these people are not Martians but my fellow men.

I could swear that I met Lawrence once, at Daniel Halévy's. Was it really he, I wonder? Someone hissed at me, "You know—the great English novelist." Well, I didn't know, and he must have noticed that my eye did not light up at the sound of his name. The fact that he was English hid him from me as if he had been behind a dense cloud or an impenetrable fog. But I do clearly remember that death was written for all to see on that drawn face; delicacy made me look away. Death —even another's—is not to be stared in the face. Was it he? I have never wanted to make sure; I've preferred the benefit of the doubt. It's too depressing to think that I could have said something to him, something like, "We're as far apart as two writers of the same age can be. And yet, my dear Lawrence, I admire you, I know all about you, and I love you. . . ."

I love him more than his books; and I love his books only to the extent that they tell me about him. What questions this man's strange destiny raises! He represents an aspect of the "social ladder" that Bourget never thought of. This miner's son became one of England's most famous writers, yet he never tried to climb socially. On the contrary, he tried to swim back upstream, like those trout with which they are hopefully stocking the brooks of Landes, although the fish find the water too warm and finally all swarm back to the cold springs. It's the same story again and again. It is the story of Maurice de Guérin and, a hundred years earlier, of young Rimbaud, the story of a man's recovering his lost dignity as a son of light. Every generation one man appears who longs to become a centaur again.

For all his living in Taos and in Mexico, Lawrence never put any silly credence in the "noble savage." I doubt that he ever expected or hoped for anything from the Indians. What he did hope was that everyone, Indian and European alike, was waiting and hoping for a revelation from him. Today, when people meet Christ—and everyone does meet Him at one time or another—they are generally either indifferent or scornful. But there is another response, which was unacknowledged until Nietzsche, which showed itself in Wilde, and which is widespread in our day. It is a spirit of rivalry or jealousy or envy. Lawrence did not want to be the Antichrist—there is no hate in Lawrence; he wanted only to be another Christ. The women who followed him were not mistaken: witness the books of Mabel Dodge Luhan, Mrs. Carswell, and Dorothy Brett, and also his biography by Alfred Fabre-Luce. For his motto, we could write the words of Jesus, hideously reversed: "What does it profit a man if he gains his soul, but suffers the loss of the whole world?" Lawrence never formulated the blasphemy in so many words, but it gives us the key to *Lady Chatterley*.

There is no vulgarity in Lawrence, no deliberate

obscenity. But this Englishman is a logician: How can man rediscover the Universe if he neglects the strength, the elemental potency of blood and flesh? If the flesh is pure, and if, contrary to Christian belief, Nature is undefiled from the beginning, who is to forbid our talking about it openly and without hypocrisy, or our using it to regain our lost paradise? Man is immoral, Lawrence says, because he has a brain. His deep instinct is pure; animals never err.

Poor Lawrence! He lived, he erred, and he died— suffocated by women, maybe; he brings to mind a book by Drieu, *L'homme couvert de femmes*. This morning, as I sit here on the terrace and watch the spring, I think about him and I wonder: is it not the same sun that shines on Taos? (The sun here is a bit more familiar, perhaps, and it does not play at being God.) Is it not the same sap that swells the plants? There are no old worlds and new worlds. The world is the same age everywhere, an Indian is no more mysterious than this old servant of my grandfather's who, from my earliest childhood, noon and night, has been fetching me a bowl of savory soup.

JEAN GIRAUDOUX

We pretend we can evaluate the work of living writers, but we know that such criticism is mostly fraudulent. The critic's art consists in commenting where he should keep quiet, in being blind to what he should see, and in ignoring obvious clues that an author scatters recklessly on every page.

Whether this voluntary blindness is practiced for reasons of charity, discretion, shame, or prudence, let's admit that without it we would have a hard time studying the breed of writer whose ideas, large and small, are conceived in the bowels and delivered from the heart. Strangely enough, the so-called "objective" writers—I mean those who do not reveal themselves in their work—almost always benefit in an equal measure from the professional discretion of the critics. Critics show them the same myopic courtesy, and belabor their work, too, in the same senseless fashion.

These things have been on my mind in connection with Jean Giraudoux, for I've been rereading two masterly scenes from *Amphitryon 38*. To the best of my knowledge, no one has ever pointed out what a raging passion inflames Giraudoux's plays. It is the same passion that fired those charming and terrible faces painted by La Tour, which, as I realized with delight every time we met, Giraudoux's own face resembled.

The author of *Electra* envelops his mockery in a cloud that recalls the devices dear to the tribe of the Encyclopedists. But our friend need not bother to mollify his most devout and Christian majesty the king nor the Jesuits nor even the indulgent M. de Malesherbes. The beautiful, many-hued cloud draped about his audacities is not designed as a protection. It is a condensation of poetry that enchants and delights its author until he forgets the passion that animates him.

What passion is this? The gods annoy him. The gods . . . but is this the point? With the single possible exception of his *Judith,* Giraudoux has never written anything for the theater more powerful than this play, which was a semi-flop on the stage. In it he was measuring himself against his true adversary, and he did not name him Jupiter but called him by his real name. He danced his terrible dance around the God of Abraham, Isaac, and Jacob—the gentle, consoling God to whom the Psalmist appealed on such an un-Giraudoux-like note: "My sacrifice, O God, is a contrite spirit; a contrite and humbled heart, O God, thou wilt not despise."

All the graceful slaps that Giraudoux lavishes elsewhere on Jupiter, are they not actually aimed at Him whom he just once (and without meanness or hate, needless to say) attacked head-on? Giraudoux's work is conceived in the spirit of the eighteenth century battling with the Angel, but in him this spirit is purified and decanted. What progress! Our latter-day Voltaire would be incapable of thinking, much less writing, "Let us crush this infamy!" We no longer find the smile hideous but charming, this smile of Jean Giraudoux.

No party in France can exploit his rich resources for their own purposes. Giraudoux is the single flower of what our pious instructors used to call the "godless" school. In its fifty-year-long search for a morality, this group has been counting on Sorbonne professors and school inspectors to discover one. Why doesn't it turn instead to this graduate of the lycée of Châteauroux who amuses himself in the playground by shooting beribboned arrows at heaven? Must I tip them off to the fact that the work—the plays especially—of Giraudoux contain a magnificent little catechism for humanists?

It is a small, earthly catechism, naturally, and one which through time and use would find itself utterly demolished. The cutting edge of Giraudoux's mind collides with a hard stone against which Greek thought before him blunted itself, the stone that we call original sin; he puts his trust in Nature and does not know that she is flawed. All the same, the little Giraudoux catechism would be a miracle. Even when pulverized by the other, its débris would be precious and useful to the sons of men.

LETTER TO FRANCIS JAMMES

Dear Jammes: I have followed a shaft of moonlight down through the black arbors to this terrace from which I look out toward you. We are separated only by the vineyards, heavy now with grapes, and by a thirty-league accumulation of fields and pine groves, of simple churches where God keeps watch, and sleeping farms. This is what you called in one of your elegies an *océan de bonté,* but it is really you, your heart and your love that break at my feet like a wave in the darkness.

You have given us this world, this murmurous night
that surrounds the bed on which you lie stretched out
in pain. The suffering poet, man's one benefactor, his
one friend! A little while ago, before I came to join
you out here on the terrace, the *Radio Journal de
France* was thundering like the voice of destiny through
the house, stilling even the laughter of children. The
boys stared at the floor as they listened. I watched the
bowed heads of my sons and the face of their friend,
which was like a sorrowing angel's. Suddenly the invisible voice uttered the terrible words announcing the
hecatomb: "Liberty, Law, Justice. . . ." When it paused,
one of the young boys near me murmured, "Just the
same . . . it would be a pity. . . ." Of what projects,
what interrupted loves was he dreaming?

Dear Jammes, great and gentle poet, your work is
the river rushing between the alders, springing without end from a hallowed heart. In you and in all men
of vision, who are your brothers, I pay honor to one
image of the goodness of God visible in this world.
Presently, when I shall have joined you who lie ill beyond the countless pines, I will be alone in a deserted
living room, in the heart of a house that shelters many
sleeps. From all over Europe music will flow into the
old room, as if it were emboldened by solitude and the
immobility of all creatures and things to offer itself
freely. Seldom does an oboe or a clarinet fail to bring
out of the air from somewhere the consolation that
Mozart lavishes on a world that stands today condemned. A line of Jammes, a melody of Mozart—

nothing more is needed to reassure us that, if mankind is plunging into the shadows where the blood of Abel has never ceased to flow, the light and joy of which you are both witness and hero none the less exist. Only in you and in your poems and in the poems of your brother poets do we sense and seek and finally discover this light, like lilacs blooming in the night.

What Frenchman is not divided against himself today? Who among us is not filled with indignation, torn between anger and shame? But you are my certitude, Jammes, you from among the very few who have not deceived us. Even in the terrible hours we are sentenced to live through, you wring from us the cry Rimbaud uttered between two blasphemies: *"Le monde est bon, je bénirai la vie. . . ."* Yes, the world is good, even if men kill each other! Yes, we will be strong enough to bless life, even as we dangle at the mercy of the whim or pleasure of a clutch of murderers.

The mighty lament that has risen from the churches and from ancient Israel, the tears and blood shed in concentration camps, the curse that has rung out from the charnel houses of Spain and Ethiopia and China, and the silence of our sons, more tragic than any outcry—these are covered, Jammes, by the piping air of your eternal song. It covers them, not to drown them nor to distract us from awareness of them but as a sign that we have not been created for cataclysm or for submission to the law of evil.

Once again I see the Bible that lies on your bed table at Hasparren. Of all those many words, these sound new and strange in our dreadful world: "Blessed are the meek, for they shall possess the earth!" It is you, O poet, who must have possessed it, for you have given it to us. You are the mild master of Béarn and the Pays Basque, of Landes and Guyenne; you reign for all time over the hills and the meadows, the streams and the springs. Fearlessly you push open the doors of old abandoned houses in farms where no one now lives; you make yourself at home in the chimney corners of dead kitchens. Your name is carved on a *prie-dieu* in the poorest village church. All that is enfolded within this night in which I write to you, all that it holds of living brooks and plants and wild hares, all the country-side that this moon bathes with light sings as it sleeps in your work, until I feel as close to you this evening as I was on a certain spring day when I opened your bedroom door.

THE SECRET OF RACINE

The war never managed to make us indifferent to everything else; despite all our anxieties, we celebrated 1940 as a Racinian year. We might even have been less mindful of Jean Racine's anniversary if we had been living enjoyably at peace, but embattled, the nation turned to him gladly, and was encouraged to recognize in him its best, if not its most popular, self. It is unlikely that we could find the complete works of Racine in farmhouses or working men's flats. But if the farmer does not know Racine, his son—the future teacher or seminary or normal school student—always comes to know him sooner or later. Hardly one family in France, no matter how humble, has not been, or is not going to be, touched by the magic of Racine.

This magic does not extend far beyond our boundaries. To foreigners, Racine is one of the least accessible of all our authors. He reigns over frontiers of the heart and mind that people who are not members of the family do not cross easily. If a foreigner says that he loves Racine and quotes a few lines in a certain tone of voice, we know that there is nothing more to explain to him about France.

To love Racine means, for most of us, to love the tragedies of Racine. The man himself remains largely unknown, and this is a sign of his literary pre-eminence, for when posterity remembers great authors as individuals it often throws their greatest works overboard. Jean-Jacques Rousseau and Chateaubriand interest us more than *Emile, La Nouvelle Héloise,* or *Natchez.* We re-read the *Confessions* of the former and *Mémoires d'outre-tombe* of the latter—that is to say, the two books that are most personally revealing. The lives these men lived hold our interest more than the novels they were able to write, and we brush aside the importunate crowd of their invented heroes to reach the protégé to whom Mme. de Warens gave lessons or the young man who was visited by a sylphid in Combourg. Take even the immense production of Voltaire; if we set aside *Ingénu* and *Candide,* what do we always go back to but the *Correspondance?* Voltaire's books charted a path for the mind of Europe, yet they matter less to us than does the old man who owed to them his amazing, his regal eminence.

This disproportion between the man and his works exists in the case of Racine, too, but here the terms are reversed. The figure of the creator is annihilated by his creation, and Jean Racine vanishes in the shadow of his great characters—some terrible, some tender—who tower above and beyond all time. For this you can take the word of an author who had the audacity, fifteen years ago, to publish a life of Racine. Of the man as he was we preserve only images as questionably authentic as the portrait that hangs in the Musée de Langres.

He is reported to have been the ungrateful friend of Molière, a ruthless rival of the elderly Corneille, the youthful lover of Du Parc. He is supposed to have suffered, in turn, at the hands of la Champmeslé. He was criticized by his colleagues and censured by the Church with equal severity. Mme. de Maintenon avers that he used to go to watch nuns take their vows because he loved to cry. According to Mme. de Sévigné, he was a Jansenist who took to loving God as passionately as he had once loved his mistresses. He was the courtier, the royal historian whose boundless devotion to the person of his sovereign was, however, less strong than his attachment to the gentlemen of Port Royal. (He died, it is said, because it fell into disgrace, although he remained faithful to his friends to the end.)

The evidence is here to choose from, to keep or discard as we will, or to accept entirely, in order to re-create the image of a man as fluid and volatile as are we all. But nothing can prevent his slipping through our fingers, no matter how we try to hold him fast. We will never stand face to face with a coherent Jean Racine whose features are as clearly drawn as those of Montaigne, for example, or Pascal.

So we are left with the alternative of searching for him in his own writing; if the plays seem to conceal him from us, it may be because the man is actually hiding in them. Perhaps Racine shouted his secret aloud while he lived, and, although we are unable to ferret him out, perhaps he is still offering it to us behind the masks of Hermione, Roxane, Phèdre, Agrippine, and Athalie.

I was first persuaded of this when I realized that heroine after heroine expresses the same desire, fury, and despair. The distance from Hermione to Roxane to Phèdre is only the difference between a passion that devours itself without divine witness and the passion that trembles before a pitiless God. I find the features of Phèdre in Athalie, a Phèdre whom age has cured of the extravagances of love, but who will gratify her other passions—her avarice, pride, cruelty, and thirst for vengeance—daring not only to stare at the sacred sun like Phèdre but to resist him with a heart full of defiance and hate.

If these formidable creatures have certain characteristics in common, if they share a kind of family likeness, might it not be that they have inherited it from the man who conceived them? One could easily extract the elements of a Racinian tragedy from the circumstances of Jean Racine's personal life that we either actually or intuitively know. Yet could we not do the same with any human being who has experienced love and betrayal, that is, do the same with almost the whole human race?

No, nothing forbids our looking for the man in his plays, as I once tried to do. On the other hand, nothing authorizes us to suppose that we can find the whole man. Racine has never given himself away. His letters would incline us to envisage him as the upright paterfamilias, the devout court poet, if we did not know that his sons, the pious Louis particularly, went to such lengths as to burn many of his papers in zeal to protect his memory. (This is standard French family procedure, and what letters we salvage are rarely those that would have yielded us the secret of the dead.)

A better reason for not taking the tragic view of Racine, if I may put it so, is supplied by Diderot. Together with the author of *Paradoxe sur le comédien,* we may legitimately believe that the artist who is too passionate, too sensitive in personal matters, is likely to be poor on stage. The creative power that can make passion real in the theater (especially to the powerful degree that Racine possessed) strongly suggests that the dramatist does not identify himself with his characters; that to depict Roxane Racine had to keep a clear head; mindful of what the great classical writers taught him, he imitated a model of passion, but he himself did not experience it.

Diderot, it is true, forgets that while an author may recover and preserve his self-possession during the act of creation, this does not exclude his more or less conscious use of memories that burn like live embers among ashes. In Racine's case, this question remains wide-open, and it would be prudent to take a middle position: the poet communicated his Christian, Jansenist lucidity to the emotions that he projected in his plays, and his understanding of them was intuitive rather than experiential.

If, after three centuries, Racine's portrait of passion still seems true in every respect, if we are not at all disconcerted by his characters' extreme preoccupation with their own feelings, we are indebted for this to Port Royal, and to generations of our moralists, but especially to our own long familiarity with Hermione, Roxane, and Phèdre. These splendid shades have escorted us through the years, from our high-school days when, in the class room, they taught us all that our devout masters strove in chapel to make us reject.

Three hundred years after the death of Jean Racine, France was to be battling a world in which the human conscience—and man himself—is in a decline, but the poet we honor today would not find this world indecipherable. The bloodiest of tyrants belong to the theatrical family of the man who depicted Nero, Agrippine, and Narcisse, and whose artistry brought all that is most inhuman within the human being out into pure light.

It is here that Racine's incomparable grandeur bursts upon us. In a France, in a Europe where nothing that he knew and cherished now survives, everything serves constantly to remind us of him, for his greatness is rooted in the human heart, which does not change. Wars and revolutions do not cut us off from the master-teachers who help us to live our lives in peacetime. They merely turn us away from mediocre minds; they hurl into oblivion what was destined for oblivion. But today, against a somber sky whose darkling clouds foretell the end of a world, the great figures from our classical art assume their full stature yet do not appear grandiose, because they are scaled to the measure of man. Today, when so many empty or inflated words fill the air, it is time for those among us who may have forgotten, to rediscover speech that is so clear and so closely attuned to the secret beating of the heart. Now is the moment to heed a logical passion that can observe itself, that can reason, and can draw from the most stringently analytic dissection of human emotion an indescribable harmony.

Having accomplished this miracle, Racine could very well turn to devote himself entirely to the service of his king and God. On April 4, 1696, he wrote to Boileau: "God has long since granted me the grace of being quite indifferent to the good or bad that may be said of my tragedies, and I remain concerned only for the account that I will some day have to render Him."

Would this Christian have achieved such detachment about his work if he had not realized its perfection? Would he have turned away so serenely from his sorely beset creatures? Racine knew perfectly well that he need not interrupt his prayers or turn for an instant from his service to the king on behalf of Andromaque, Bérénice, or Phèdre. His heroines no longer needed him; they had nothing to fear from anyone. Within his own lifetime they had crossed the threshold of immortality and they belonged henceforth to France— that is to say, to that which shall not perish.

PART TWO: LIFE

1. *The First Day of the Year*

THE FIRST DAY OF THE YEAR

Even as a child I did not believe that the first day of the year was like all other days. The pavements seemed to exhale a special smell. Mysterious rays of light filtered through the fog of the city. Beggars at street corners rejoiced in their luck as they resold their holiday gifts. Family reunions fairly smothered one, and group games monopolized the full width of the pavements. New toys intoxicated the children and made them blissfully impervious to a storm of kisses unleashed by hordes of second cousins.

Even today it is useless for me to remind myself that this day was chosen from among all others by a mere pact among men. I find it impossible to work, impossible to read, for here in the room with me is the tall, veiled figure of the unknown year.

A Roman ambassador used to conceal his message of

war or peace in the folds of his toga. Similarly, the destiny of the world and of each one of us lurks under the mantle drawn around the still faceless year. We should not be so much concerned to know if war or peace, disgrace or glory, is hidden in these dark folds, or even to know if our greatest adventure, our own death, will take place at dawn or dusk on a particular day out of the three hundred and sixty-five that lie ahead. For the folds of the cloak do not conceal from us the one thing that counts, which is how we are inwardly prepared to welcome this silent phantom. This depends only on ourselves. This day is the day for each of us to assess our own strength, in utter silence to plumb the depths of our own spirit.

Most men resemble great deserted palaces: the owner occupies only a few rooms and has closed off wings where he never ventures. But on this day he dares tiptoe into those shadowy apartments; he opens shutters; he looks to see where this fetid smell comes from, notices that here or there the roof is leaking.

May the immense unknown of this New Year find no weakness in us. All that is already stirring under the half-parted cloak is a danger that threatens, the still unknown pain as well as the pleasure that debases and the success that blights. We must be prepared to accept pain, pleasure, and success—to accept them without perishing in them.

II

The simplest and, in my view, the most appropriate way of approaching the New Year is to welcome it in a spirit of meditation, but many people shrink from this. They find even poison palatable if it helps them to be oblivious of time and blind to the milestones that mark its passing. They are not anxious to know what the folds of the New Year's mantle conceal from them, because whatever happens, for better or for worse, they have resolved to ignore it.

Today for instance an immense and growing portion of humanity sits brutishly drugged in the shadow of death. We can no longer dismiss the problem of their addiction as one confined largely to Asia, for, even though unknown to us, the victims of narcotics are all around us. We would undoubtedly be appalled if we knew how many narcotic addicts there are.

These unhappy people care nothing about the New Year, for even time itself does not concern them. They are partisans as it were of escape. They have left the train that carries the rest of us onward, and are persuaded that they have successfully evaded the fatality of events. Actually, they have only created a new fatality by surrendering to an obscure and terrifying power. The simple joys and sorrows that the New Year hides under its cloak to distribute among the children of men are tuppence toys, not designed for these explorers of false paradises; set aside for them are custom-built games of madness, murder, and suicide. How many young criminals who appear before our juries are drug addicts! How many suicides have been addicts! To people who have elected to live as sleepwalkers, what can the New Year matter? They no longer belong to the realm of time but to eternity, and what a fearful eternity! Their dark Master is the immortal angel of death.

But those of us who still have hope will wait without fear for the mantle to part, however slowly it does so. Whatever trembles under its folds, whether joy or grief, will be welcomed with love. We are engaged in a game that we cannot help but win. We hold a secret that transmutes every defeat into victory. The stakes in the game of life have already been delivered into our hands: *"Pax Dei quae exsuperat omnem sensum. . . ."* We have won the game before it starts.

Yet during this night vigil it will profit us to contemplate the great form of the New Year as it draws near, wrapped in still unknown events and necessities. We will do well to plumb the depths of our life during the past year to discover what lessons it holds for us. How long life seems when we enumerate all the things that over twelve months have befallen us: what a crowd of casual circumstances and crises, bereavements, illnesses, obscure threats to the flesh, all the failures and successes, as well as those other dramas that are played out in the depths of a human soul! There, perhaps, storms were unleashed that did not stir even the surface of our lives and that God intervened to quiet. Let us dare on this great night to descend into those hidden regions where lie the conquered passions, the misshapen monsters, and the half-stifled memories.

2. The Ages of Man—and Woman

CHILD MARTYRS

Every morning at breakfast, the newspapers announce the newest child martyr—the martyr for the day. The public indignation aroused by stories of violence and crime is certainly legitimate, especially the indignation of mothers. And yet we should look one very unpleasant fact in the face: the world loves children much less than it thinks it does. All the waifs and strays in the movies and the storybooks would soften no hearts if they were not pretty.

I remember making my debut as an observer of the human race at the age of five or six. I had ripped my eyelid while playing, and until it healed, I felt that it made me most unprepossessing to look at; during this period I discovered a connection between my getting the lowest examination marks in my whole class and my unhappy appearance. Life was to develop my tendency to see things in terms of absolutes, but even before that, I had established it as a general rule that the head of the class always had the curliest hair.

I knew quite well that people were already saying about me, "This child always exaggerates. . . ." Yet it is true that we do not love children; we love the pretty ones, so pretty that we "could eat them up."

Children are quick to understand that the important thing for them is to be neat and well-behaved in order to please us. Their coquetry and their conscience are awakened simultaneously. They are initiated early into their job of charming that monster known as a grownup. In the first years of school, what a game of flattery they play with their teachers! Later, they get some of their own back, when they have the upper hand and can cut up as much as they like. But for the first four or five years, how dutifully they laugh at the stupidest jokes of authorities, just as they gang up with the powers that be against the scapegoat.

The scapegoat is never handsome—or, if so, his is a hidden beauty that escapes the bullies. The child victim is adorable only in the films. You wouldn't like David Copperfield to squint and to have pimples, would you? Bullies make martyrs of the young as they do of the old, and for the same reasons: in both cases, unfortunately, when the person is unhappy, he is at once repugnant and defenseless. The child and the old man are always sick, they cry at night, they soil their beds. Little as they eat, they themselves bring nothing in. A child is unbearable because he is always there. In the slums of Paris and London where the human couple

lives like the animals, the child is witness to their battles and embraces, to the whole dismal brawl from
which he himself has issued.

Often a man smothers his own child the way he
would smother his conscience. For that matter, the pitiful little witness is often a stranger to the parent: the
father sees in him the woman who has vanished, leaving this miserable creature behind her. But a small
body is too weak to have to bear the anger of a harsh
stepmother and a flouted husband. And then, too, the
parent is a slave, a helot crushed by the social pyramid,
with no one lower than he except this puny creature
who is utterly in his power. An immense, pent-up bitterness, an incalculable reserve of hatred has only the
innocent child on which to vent itself.

Are people who maltreat children monsters? Certainly, but in my *Petit Larousse* the example that I
find under the word "scapegoat" is, "The cabin boy
was formerly the scapegoat of the crew." What more
need be said? . . . Let us have the courage to admit it:
the scapegoat has always had the mysterious power of
unleashing man's ferocious pleasure in torturing, cor-
rupting, and befouling.

What makes one shudder is the realization that the
press reports only extreme cases. Where does discipline
stop? Where does cruelty begin? Somewhere between
these two, thousands of children inhabit a voiceless
hell.

Let us add that the State (and the State is each of us)
which passes laws to restrain or punish unsuitable par-

ents is itself a child-butcher in its reformatories. Everyone knows that this is a fact. Must it be so? Must the scapegoat be kept in irons so long as human life endures, and submit interminably to torments that he does not understand?

TIME FLIES—OR DOES IT?

What do people do to fill up their days? A day is a long time, even for men with big, responsible jobs. It is longer still for the artists, since inspiration does not visit them every hour on the hour. But none of this prevents everyone from appearing to be very busy. A man never sees his friends and writes: "My dear fellow, how time flies! We never see each other. . . ." We don't see each other because we have no wish to see each other.

This is the difference between the friends of our youth and the friends of our maturity. To love someone at twenty means, first of all, trusting and giving oneself to him freely; at fifty it all too often means lunching occasionally in a restaurant with some young man who wants a favor and from whom we expect something in return. To say that trust no longer obtains is an understatement.

The friend looks at his watch and exclaims, "Two o'clock already! I have to run. . . ." Where is he running? Where is everyone hurrying? What is the stuff of which our destiny is made? What do we really know of the people we feel we know best? All of a sudden they emerge from the mystery that is their secret life, dressed for the evening, complete with flower and smile. A terrible language is obscurely traced on their worn faces in letters that we will never decipher. Unknown to them, some mysterious disk must have recorded every word they have said, some film registered every thing they have done since morning. . . . This is one of the most terrifying of God's aspects—this sensitive plate on which everything is indelibly impressed for all eternity.

It is not the important job, not even the important work of creative art, that takes up time; it is the passions. Remove from any life the passion of love or of holiness, and you will be appalled by how little remains.

It is generally agreed that a doctor or surgeon or lawyer never has time enough. But that part of them which is expended in great activity does not involve their innermost selves. The figure sitting behind the desk who listens to you, indeed, who listens carefully and takes notes, is the lawyer or the doctor but not the man himself; that figure is not the same person who presently will lean against a door to catch the sound of the approaching elevator, or who will slip into a dark church to sit in silence until the doors must be closed.

No doubt the inner mystery diminishes as life runs out. For many old people only the social function survives; the uniform, the honorary robe, the rows of medals are all that is left. These are the people whom old age has defeated. Many of them exhibit some dreadful little mania, the residue of outworn passion, that— depending on our temperament— amuses or revolts us. But true passion is not ridiculous at any age. I see nothing comical, for instance, in Goethe's last love affair or in the last desire of Chateaubriand.

It is not true that men hide only the worst of themselves. Not every secret is shameful. One must hope to grow old keeping one's life and background richly filled, hope to live so that people need us and we need them until the end. Nothing, of course, can prevent old age from being a desert, an expanse of sand that gradually covers and smothers everything. But it is for us to preserve enough strength to plant and people our desert, to create oases in the midst of our solitude.

The *Cahiers* of Barrès show how concerned he was to marshal all his resources against the dark years that lay ahead and that only death would end. Who knows? Perhaps he would have grown gentle as an old man, even though he was cruel when he was young, cruel but nevertheless capable of kindness and, even more, of delicacy, and, as a mature man, iron-jawed indeed. At forty, he was bored, and used to say, "If I didn't have the Chamber . . ." Perhaps now his days would be all too short.

What an achievement to have a full old age! Above all, we must not run after what has always eluded us, not try to keep up with the young but be content when they come to us. And if no one comes? I look at old men sitting in cafés. They had more toys when they were children. Some go to classes, repeating the courses that they cut at twenty; they visit museums where once upon a time a girl waited for them; they leaf through old newspapers in the libraries; and, at a certain point in the afternoon, they collapse in front of little marble tables in the cafés only to have their pleasure in their apéritif spoiled because they keep thinking of their blood pressure.

And if they have married children and grandchildren, there is the given day and hour for visiting. Better to stay away except for that established day and hour. Not that one would not be glad to see them, but . . .

THE AGE OF SUCCESS

By the time a man notices that he is no longer young, his youth has long since left him. He has been deluded by a flickering of passion, buoyed up by his animal drive. Occasionally, as he has faced his shaving mirror in the morning, he has felt a twinge of uneasy surprise. Temples turning a little white, eh? Bags under the eyes? But he has quickly repaired the damage, using as his model the young man whose image he preserves intact in his mind.

We do not really see ourselves. All mirrors are in fact quite useless except the living, human mirrors who reflect us: they do not lie.

Other people's feelings for us do not diminish, do

not become more straitened as we grow older; on the contrary, they become more complicated. A man such as the one I have in mind could have noted on his calendar the exact day when he first noticed in a younger companion's attitude and tone of voice a touch of deference, a shade of respect. And from that day on, he found the same signs wherever he looked, precisely as if all his juniors had passed the word around.

This man had certainly not reached the age when his contacts with others had to depend largely upon some occasion such as autographing books, or writing a preface, or adding a postscript to some letter of recommendation, or, even more simply, paying his monthly bills. But let us say that young women, who had always been gay and easy in his company, were beginning to talk to him about Proust with disquieting persistence. An author discovers this dubious gift of maturity gradually. There was a time when he had only to shy away from those who are bores either by birth or by profession; now, it seems, he conjures them up; somehow he creates them by the way he looks, and, further, the moment he appears, the most delightful women suddenly turn "serious."

They no longer see the man, they see the celebrity he has become. "You have become someone" is a compliment that touches the older man while leaving him slightly bemused; his problem is to live inside this "someone" and not to be suffocated by him. "You have arrived. . . ." Arrived where? In Parliament? In the Ministry? In the Institute? Everyone gets off the train somewhere; the problem is to set off continually on a fresh journey—not to sit down on one's luggage, not to doze off in some way station of success.

With age, there is a strong temptation, even for the man who is not venal, to stop trying, to sit down at table and consent to be the established personality others see in him. He tells himself that this semi-official presence to which the world pays homage is scarcely any less his real self than the sought-after young man he once was. A young man is rarely loved for his spirit but usually for the fugitive light that touches him briefly, no more and no less than millions of other men. The importance of the man who is forty, the air he displaces, the space he occupies, differentiate him, set him apart from the crowd: he sits in full view, squarely in the limelight. Youth, on the other hand, confuses and blinds us and prevents our seeing. Women do not become real to us until they reach middle age; when they are younger, they interpose between us and their true feelings a mist of charm such as few men can penetrate. That is why the women who were most deeply loved were the least known—and why so many love stories end unhappily.

As a result, the older man tries to find some comfort in disparaging the young; indeed, he discovers many other sophisms to sanction the fact that he is nothing but a celebrity dozing in the midst of success, pretending that he feels happy and cherished. He naps. . . . But often this is also the moment when he hears a little warning note and, in spite of himself, he is kept wide awake. Something is happening, he does not know quite what, somewhere in his body. . . . It can be nothing at all, something so slight that he cannot describe the symptoms to a doctor. It is not even a pain; he simply "feels his heart beat." He cannot keep from noticing the beat; it is irregular and too strong; he cannot stop thinking that this pulsation has never been interrupted, day or night, for half a century.

Sometimes it is a question of a more specific disorder; the doctor hesitates, hints at something or other, and the words he does not say are promptly written in letters of fire on the walls of his office. Outside a streetcar clangs, a record is being played in the next room. This time "it" concerns me—the "it" that did not exist for me, I thought, only for the others. As the moralist says: the death that I cannot look in the face is my own; the death of others I have always fixed courageously with my eye, without any need for dark glasses.

II

Lo, the sleeper is awake. This time "it" is for him, for him alone.

The man who has arrived, no matter what heights he may have reached, discovers that what he finally comes to is the waiting room where we all end up— and he watches the door that opens on the void of eternity swing back and forth in the wind. A hand rests on his shoulder, gently at first, but then it clutches his heart or paralyzes his legs or grips his throat. . . . He is still alive, he is quite safe, but he will never sleep

again. He scarcely wants to. He cares very little now
that people know only the more or less ornate façade
of his "success." His prison is no longer a prison but a
cell—what Catherine of Siena called "the cell of self-
knowledge." As he gains the courage to remain in it
alone, the more worthy he becomes to discover a presence there. It is when he thinks that everything is finished, when the world is perhaps already saying that he
is finished, that he has a sense of beginning, of being
born.

Yet, on the outside his public personality will continue
to go through the necessary motions; it will perform its
duties with ease and promptness and, in a word, with
the alacrity of the good servant who anticipates his
master's wishes. I have no idea if overtaxed men ever
pray, in their own fashion, but they could do so without
even interrupting the prudent game they play. For that
matter, the external freedom of action of these great
politicians has been much reduced; their party, the
public sphere in which they move, and a thousand con-
tingencies allow them only a narrow margin of influence on events. And so it is for each of us: it is within
ourselves that we remain free; there the one drama
that we have the right to direct is played out. Who
could dream that he was master of the universe? But
the least among men is, until his death, the master
of his own soul.

SATIETY

"It isn't true, life is not short!" She was still young, but she spoke with a certain urgency. "Think how long I have been beautiful! When I look in the mirror, I can see that my face has not changed in all these years. And it will stay this way, it will stay . . . stay. . . ."

I listened to the despair in the voice. I looked at the childlike face. It was quite unmarred by time, but it bore the brand of a curse; it seemed to be saying that there is nothing so sad as to be surfeited with pleasure, that satiety is a sickness.

How many women seem to have had bestowed on them every gift that life can offer, yet they suffocate in a solitude against which they have no defense left but sleep? Thanks to a kind of infernal grace, no excess ever mars their incorruptible youthfulness. They are spared every trial, even the tribulation all other human beings share: age. Incurably young, according to the world incurably fortunate, they are protected by a special privilege so inexorable that they come to fear it. This kind of woman helps us to understand why we are denied what we ask for; truly it is the afflictions that God sends us that are the measure of His love.

These incurably lucky ones are almost always fated to be alone. They do not attract hearts that know what it is to suffer. They have nothing to give, and there is nothing they can accept. What a desert of luxury!

A film of frost, a sheet of ice sheathes and isolates them. A man has to look at these overdressed, overly made-up women through a glittering and inviolable casing.

Yet sometimes mortal love becomes for them the instrument of Grace, God's right-hand man of God; love shatters the shell, destroys the false happiness, disturbs the false peace, dissipate the false youthfulness, ferrets out the creature as she crouches amid her comforts, and unseals her tears. And she, believing that she is driven to despair, does not yet know that she has been made whole.

If those who are sore beset sometimes look enviously at one of these brilliant, seemingly blessed creatures, let let them remember that what the world calls happiness is often a trial without reward, a sterile sufferance, a shining but deserted isle ruled by satiety: a fatal affliction.

AN INTERVIEW WITH GRETA GARBO

Greta Garbo seems to me a kind of deer relentlessly pursued by a pack of journalists baying at her heels. She has left luggage behind her in hotels to throw the bloodhounds off the scent; she has many times cowered in secret hideaways. Last night, however, in a dream, Greta Garbo opened the door to my study, walked into the room and sat down across from me, as if she had come for an interview—a thing that was all the more strange since I have never been one of her hunters.

It was toward the end of a November day; the shutters

were still open, but the lamps had already been lighted. I could not see her face very clearly, yet I knew it was she. Perhaps I should have gotten up and offered a suitable welcome to such a famous beauty. I didn't. I lay on my couch and did not say a word. Any gesture of welcome would have seemed as crazy as if, while I sat in some movie house, my lips had tried to pursue those beautiful hands of hers across the screen.

Miss Garbo began talking to me. Without preamble, she begged me not to think badly of her for hating interviews so. Her motives, she insisted, were not selfish ones. It wasn't that she cared only for her own comfort, she said, it wasn't even a need for rest and privacy that made her so elusive. "Try to understand me, Monsieur," she said, almost pleadingly. "Imagine how often I have sat way in the back of some theater—whether in New York, Chicago, Vienna, Berlin, or Paris doesn't matter—and in the hazy half-light watched the enormous crowd fascinated by my face. It's always the same crowd—or, rather, as it seems to me, the same captive monster from which floats up like incense toward my face the smoke from thousands and thousands of cigarettes.

"My face—" she paused. "The terrible thing is, all those rapt eyes are devouring a face that isn't mine, that is not my real face. Mine is bruised and stained with kisses and tears, it's even a little lined. Pain and grief, you know, leave a mark on any face, no matter how beautiful or cherished it is.

"But the public doesn't dream that what they see

isn't my real face. Even I have forgotten what it's like. I've had to change the face God gave me as a child in order to offer pepole the ageless miracle they worship on the screen. . . . Who can tell whether I have eye-brows that are truly mine? Even I can't. My lashes—they're very famous, but are they real, are they mine? My body is still young, of course, but even I can't be sure that it's alive and warm. How could it be, through all the creams and powder and paint? . . . Perhaps, Monsieur, I have destroyed myself. I sometimes feel that I have sacrificed my real self to become an image: the image of a beautiful woman who can gratify each of thousands of hopeless expectations and frustrated desires. The real Greta Garbo has been transformed into the vision of what the adolescent will never find, what the middle-aged man has spent fifty futile years searching for, what this woman or that wishes desper-ately she were so that she could hold on to the man who is slipping away from her. Now, Monsieur, do you see why I hide? I hide out of pity for all these people, for all of them, because I don't want them to know that I do not really exist."

This is what Greta Garo said to me: she confessed that she did not really exist. As I listened, I intuitively understood, half accepted what she said, yet there she sat and with my own eyes I saw her. Or rather, in the uncertain evening light, I glimpsed the marvelous out-line of her features. She had marvelous features, yet they were not, I observed, too unlike many others. The short veil stopping just above her mouth hid what little was not already invisible under the layer of paint that coats all womankind today. It struck me as strange that the cinema requires its stars to wear such excessive make-up in order to project to us the pure essence of a face. The mysterious barrier of the screen lets only the imperishable elements of nose and mouth filter through. Perhaps the paints and salves help to absorb and dissolve all the ephemeral parts. Perhaps, too, God's intent in creating such a face shows forth in the heavenly simplicity of this design, cleansed of all stains, readied as if for Eternity. I could understand how anyone in the world would be tempted to fall to his knees before such a vision, such a revelation, if the screen, unfortunately, did not also isolate and emphasize and rivet our eyes on the dangerous appeal that exists for each of us in too great beauty.

A feverishly susceptible boy, lost in the countless crowds of moviegoers, must in his solitude struggle with the immense turmoil Greta Garbo's marvelous eyes arouse in him. Desire is secretly stirred by this woman who is so real, even though she is also inaccessible. She smiles, she parts her lips, she arches her neck, she half closes her eyes. All these things she does with impunity. She is vibrant, "present" in the fullest physical sense, offered to millions of men; yet if one of them were to be seized by frenzy and rush toward her, he would find a piece of cloth stretched across a space—the rag that decoys the bull—and he would embrace emptiness. Does Greta Garbo know, perhaps, that on a certain evening, in Philadelphia or in Buenos Aires or in Melbourne, one of her nameless lovers suddenly started up from his seat and ploughed his way through a mass of furious bodies, trampling on the crowd as if he were walking on water? Does she know that he reached for that figure, visible but forever beyond his grasp, and with a ripping of cloth plunged headfirst through the screen? . . . It is a strange scene to imagine, yet it recalls a line of Rimbaud: *"Puis, o désespoir, la cloison devint vaguement l'ombre des arbres, et je suis abimé sous la tristesse amoureuse de la nuit. . . ."*

"Yes," Greta Garbo admitted in a low voice, "I have unleashed that kind of madness, I know, and I am afraid of it. It is fear, too, which makes me shun people. I have been unfaithful to millions of men; I have indeed betrayed all mankind. I ask myself about this flood of humanity, this carnal ocean that fills the dark caves of the film houses night and day and is renewed hour after hour—I wonder won't it someday spew forth someone, some boy perhaps, bent on revenge?

"Of course," she went on, as if to reassure herself, "he would never recognize me. He would not dare strike a woman who looks like any other woman. He would see that in real life I am not the Greta Garbo he knows, that I don't look at all like the star in the movie magazines he reads."

Greta Garbo sat in silence before me. Her magical eyes looked at me, begging for some word of comfort, and I thought how only the cinema puts men at the mercy of our eternal adversary; it removes all the cares that engulf and disarm women in daily life and that make real women less dangerous. Only at the films can we understand the full meaning of those lines of de Vigny:

Et les rois d'Orient ont dit dans leurs cantiques
Ton regard redoutable à l'égal de la mort . . .

"Have you ever thought," I asked Miss Garbo, "that a great many crimes may be committed because of you? It is hard for a young man of feeling to go back to his drab routine after an evening at a movie, an evening spent in dreaming he has been with you. And while the ostentatious luxury of the films is an abomination, still your face makes the abomination almost irresistibly appealing. It's ironic, isn't it, that we should call it 'high life' when it is the lowest, most abject thing in the world? But you are so beautiful that a boy's brief spree can appear altogether glamorous. The poor fellow —he forgets about his philosophers and his poets and all the things he treasures, to dream that he is some broad-shouldered, athletic hero swaggering into an expensive restaurant behind a woman whose name is magic, and that the whispers fly from table to table: 'Greta Garbo! Look, that's Greta Garbo!' "

I saw Miss Garbo's body sag in the shadows, and she dropped her head. The lamp lighted her pale gold hair. "No, don't," I said. "You're wrong to hide your face. This mountain—better, this sea—of adoration and desire that batters against your multiplied image does not rise from an impure source. Millions of hearts cherish you because they know instinctively that truth is not found in the words of the philosophers or in the formulas of learned men. They know that truth is not abstract but carnal and alive, and that it is possible for them to find it and meet it and talk to it; they know that truth is *Someone*. Like you, truth has a forehead, a glance, a voice, a heart—a name among all other names. Saint John attested to this when he wrote of 'What we have heard, what we have seen with our eyes, what we have looked upon and our hands have handled . . .'

"You occupy the place of that Presence, and your face hides its absence, for you are a replacement, a double, a reflection. You give the lie to man's hunger and thirst for beauty, and that is why you can hold the miserable human herd motionless before a screen. Yet, and this is what *I* have often dreamed, think of the beauty and the magic of those other Features, of that other celestial, dazzling Face were it suddenly to appear on a piece of cloth stretched before the fascinated multitudes in all the movie palaces of this world!"

THE SLEEPWALKERS

No sooner are they inside the door for the party than it is one, two, three cocktails for a fast pickup, and so it goes until the inevitable last "quick one for the road." This pattern has not yet succeeded in reducing everyone to sodden silence, especially not in Paris, where that delightful even if old-fashioned custom of sparkling conversation still survives, thank Heaven. You can still meet quite a few people of the kind once admiringly described as "wits," though unfortunately in some circles, jazz has already begun to drown them out.

Alcohol lends the faces of its prisoners, young and old alike, a certain vivacity, a curiously mindless animation. They are drained of all spiritual substance, or rather, they appear to be, for the spirit is still there even if bound and gagged somewhere inside them. Now and then it breaks free; a fugitive smile will brighten a young face leaning over some shoulder . . . but it is quickly gone. Such brief resurrections are rare in the women, who have, so to speak, remade their faces to a point where the face bears no relation to the spirit, the spirit finds no way to express itself in the face. How poorly protected they must feel by these masks that are forever in need of being touched up and repaired! Yet the elderly woman who has tinted her hair blue—the exact blue, incidentally, of the sulphate I spray on my grapevines—can dance serenely on; what joy or despair could possibly lurk under her indigo curls?

One wonders if all these jazz-deafened creatures are indifferent to each other. Are the people they love somewhere else? Without doubt, in many cases they are. Perhaps some come to the party to forget an intoxication or an agony which the members of their circle know nothing about, an enchantment no one suspects, a despair that has its source elsewhere. Theirs must be a clandestine happiness. It is concealed in some other world, at an opposite pole, in a world where faces are

nakedly exposed—or besmeared so coarsely with paint
that nothing about the loved one is revealed.

But others at this party are lovers, and this is their
favorite rendezvous. Here they can enjoy the animal
pleasure of being together without the deception of
speech. They have learned to isolate and quarantine
speech, as if it were a germ. No more discussions, no
more explanations are required. Alcohol eliminates any
need to communicate and, in any case, the music alone
would make it impossible. They have given up the
frantic search to discover the exact nature of the love
they inspire and to compare it with the love they themselves feel—all that is so much nonsense, well enough
in books, but they want no more of it.

Existence for these people is a kind of sleep that is
willed and induced, a collective renunciation of the
mind. They are weary of pain, they have reached the
limits of their endurance, they can stand no more.
They aspire to the supreme luxury of unconsciousness,
yet love, too, must somehow be made to fit in. The
trick is to enjoy love without the suffering Proust speaks
of: "How does one have the courage to want to be
alive, how can one make any effort to fend off death
in a world where love is born of a lie and consists only
of our need to have our anguish appeased by the creature who has made us suffer?"

This is the agony that these people are trying to
escape. Alcohol they know how to abuse with discretion,
if I may put it so; it initiates them into silence. Not the
vital silence that leaves the mind active, not even the

silence of innocent animals ruminating in a dark stable. Theirs is a kind of half-death: pain is numbed; despair is held at arm's length, but it is still there, prowling about and sniffing behind the door.

Male and female, they sit side by side, drink, and are silent. They no longer know anything about each other, not even each other's age. (The question of age doesn't arise, since they can erase all signs of growing old. Age corrodes women on the inside now; it has become an inner malady.)

They have discovered that all their suffering came from the restless seeking of two hearts that meet but neither beats in the same rhythm nor even stands still at the same moment. If they no longer give to each other, it is because they have lost all hope of being paid back in kind. Why go through the wearisome bother of asking questions that receive only ambiguous answers? These couples have done with the eternal "Do you still love me?" They decline the comforts of deception. They are quite content to be blind to the finer shades of feeling in their partners and are even indifferent to what they themselves feel. "Know thyself": this they think is a kind of poison. Henceforth, in reaction to a Freud and a Proust, it seems that lovers want merely to bow their heads under the same yoke and bend over the trough of a chrome-and-mahogany bar.

Yet the majority of them have preserved one lively preoccupation: they worry about décor. The setting for their blessed state of non-being must be quite correct.

Bare walls (nothing is allowed that could arouse or arrest a thought or provoke an opinion) welcome the light; it is an intense light as hostile to any mystery as it is restful to dulled eyes and stilled hearts. Contrary to what they sometimes assume, this modern style, so clean and so stripped, is not always expressive of a youthful, realistic, dynamic society; it sometimes expresses a world that is literally stupefied and, like a mollusk, secretes this bland shell to shelter an altogether torpid existence.

It is a fearful torpor. These people are far more adept than the rest of us at defending themselves against God, against the knowledge of suffering that has been and remains for many the bait of conversion. For that matter, why should these unfortunates trouble themselves to search for *anything?* They have discovered a kind of besotted tranquility, and they never ask if it is not more grievously reprehensible than the quivering alertness aroused by passion, even if sinful.

Blessed are they for whom love remains what Claudel calls "this sword through the heart," and who need never seek this death in life.

A VISIT TO PORT ROYAL

During a Sunday visit to Port Royal, two young people who accompanied me were quite annoyed, as I would have been at their age, by the crowd that invaded the solitude of the site. Advancing age must now and again give us a compensatory sense of being the richer for our years, for I found myself touched rather than irritated by these noisy visitors to a shrine of my youth.

Several intense young people were sitting on the grass around a lecturer who, with great fire and finesse, was expounding the nature of man according to the teaching of Saint Augustine. I was drawn to them but also felt a bond with the people who were merely strolling through this small valley, quite unaware that it had once been the scene of a stirring drama of the spirit.

I should have liked to say to them: "Everything that could be done to destroy this place by force has in fact been done. Not one stone of this famous abbey was left standing on another, graves were violated, the ashes of the dead were scattered. You know nothing, perhaps, about this story. Nevertheless see how you are still responsive to a presence, to a message that somehow endures here."

It was admittedly a heresy that sprang from this valley, and the heresy was rightly condemned. But error was uprooted with such abominable violence that it became in a certain sense equivalent to truth itself: for when erroneous belief is held in good faith, even to the point of heroic virtue and at the price of one's life, it undoubtedly shares in the nature of truth.

The tyrants' role has always been to join, by a river of blood, if necessary, pure and indisputable truth with alleged truths which we do not believe to be pure and in which we can in fact observe some imperfection.

Hitler's sole mission in the world, if viewed in this light, was to teach men divided by doctrine and race that they can respond to the same hate only because they respond to the same love.

As I reflected that this was the very spot on our earth where, on a certain night, Pascal exchanged with his God words that still kindle men's hearts, I told myself that all the evil to come from Port Royal des Champs was compensated for by this testimony, by Blaise Pascal's conversation with the Saviour, by this one man's meeting with his God. I mean specifically Pascal's conversation with *his* God, not with the God of Calvin or Jansenius, nor with the Divine Being as conceived by this or that Church Father, but with God as He manifests Himself in speaking to each one of us, when He takes His place in the center of an obscure life story, the humble drama of an individual man. In the wake of Pascal's conversation with his God, angry men knocked down walls, violated tombs, and scattered ashes, until nothing remained but the poplars, the tall grass, and the wind. Yet centuries later, on this clear Sunday in June, we can still hear the adorable reply that Pascal heard here, one November evening: "I have loved thee more ardently than thou hast loved thy sins."

Louis XIV did not know that here, in this Port Royal ravaged by his grave-despoilers, the two voices of man and of God would continue to speak to each other among the boughs, and that his Spanish zeal to exhume the remains of sleeping nuns would never interrupt the dialogue of fire. "With every manner of indecency," as an historian put it, those holy bodies, some of them still in their habits, were tossed into heaps for the dogs to prowl around. This horrible crime was committed, strangely enough, on the exact anniversary of the night when Pascal wept for joy.

Today the seasons reign over the wild valley that, in the unforgettable words of the Marquis de Pomponne, "had the misfortune to displease His Majesty." While the unrecoverable ashes of those victims await the Resurrection, I sat there, a little removed from the Sunday crowds strolling on the June grass that blanketed a now peaceful earth.

Why was it that, on the way home, I was haunted, not by any word spoken there, but by something the Spanish saint, John of the Cross, said a century before Pascal in a phrase wonderfully calculated to move us and also, if we have understood its powerful fascination, to terrify us: *"Au soir de cette vie, vous serez jugés sur l'amour."*

It is true that love sometimes impels us to unjust violence. Pascal himself, like every man who builds or founds something, even if by fire and sword, knows that he is not moved by hate alone. Perhaps the last ruse of mercy will be to discover in our wildest frenzies, in all our excesses and abuses of power, a spark or reflection of eternal love.

3. On War

The swarming flies hum like a human crowd, or like the dull roar of a riot or of the ocean; between branches and sky, they sound the lament of a mindless world.

This is the siesta hour, when a man scarcely feels free to refuse sleep. One should go indoors and enjoy the cretonne freshness of the couch against one's cheek. But Paris, which I left only forty-eight hours ago, still buzzes in me too, with all *its* flies. From right and left, they assail me—the patriots who do not really love their country, the pacifists who do not really love peace, the intellectuals adept at making logic serve their passions, the theologians who dangle crime on a hangman's rope of syllogisms.

I must stop thinking of such things. This old house (how many people now dead have loved it!) is surrounded by fruit trees that must be propped up this year, so laden are they with peaches and plums. The grapes, already bunched, thrust their way through the sprayed leaves. A mild breeze bears their fragrance up to me; this scent of sun-warmed vines is blended in memory with the burning melancholy of a summer vacation when I was seventeen.

I did not know then that some measure of happiness is possible. It is agonizing to see and to sense, as now I do, that man could be happy; no doubt it would be a happiness threatened by worry and grief, but the trials and the joys would all be within a human dimension.

The travail that threatens us now has not been cut to any human measure. A few men forbid us to live our true life. Which men? Those who pretend that they incarnate the dominating spirit of a race, its will to power. Indeed, although the yeast of their pride swells the obedient masses, they impose disproportionate goals on countless young people who dream of play and bread, of work and love, but not of empire; they substitute for humble and simple human desires their own insane and terrible fantasies.

How strange it is that the destiny of a nation may be bound not so much to the will as to the whim of one man! The fleeting vagaries of one individual are engraved forever in the history of his people. And thus a ravenous Germany finds herself suddenly and irrevocably yoked to an underfed Italy.

Let me brush away the flies that drive off sleep, and empty my mind of these thoughts. Let the vast hum of summer enfold me and rock and cradle me until the hour comes for the shadows to lengthen. Let me learn to sleep in this fiery furnace, so that I may keep awake late into the night. For even dusk is stifling. Even after the god has vanished behind the three crosses of Verdelais, the earth still exhales sunshine, and one must wait for the relief of the first breath of air to come from who knows what moist paradise.

I am going to lie down on the far side of the house, where a few ancient elms have survived the terrible blight of these last years. Their yellowed crests seem to beseech the northern constellations. None of my desires, nor my sense of outrage, nor my lamentations have any more influence on the course of events during the brief moment of my restless tossing here on earth than have the stricken branches of these last few elms on the course of the stars as they reach imploringly to heaven.

SOLITUDE DURING THE WAR

I remember an infantryman at the camp outside Châlons, during the First World War, who confessed, "For me the hardest thing in the trenches is the loneliness." For some people, war means an intensified loneliness. Camaraderie is of no help to them.

Loneliness belongs in a way to God, too. Someone said once that such and such a thing we had done was "not like" us. There are times when history is "not like" our Father who is in Heaven, so powerfully does violence prevail over Grace. The Catholic nations are perishing one after another, not only physically but because their spirit has been delivered over to dictators who possess tried and true means for killing Christ in young hearts. The masters of Russian Poland and the masters of German Poland have a game they play together: which will dechristianize the country faster?

But temperaments like those I speak of feel that infinitely more than their own spirit has been deserted: "Why hast thou forsaken me?" This is God crying to God.

Wherever we may be, we must manifest our faith in a redoubled closeness to our comrades who endure this test of inner solitude and abandonment. If we have received a greater measure of hope, we must share it with those who are poorer. This has nothing to do with forced optimism and the official "the-situation-is-developing-according-to-plan," which is precisely what these people fear most. They ask only that we be attentive, that even more than to answer them we know how to listen to them. Above all, let us be wary of ready-made ideas about cowardice and courage: the same burden weighs infinitely more heavily on some shoulders than on others.

Do not judge: during a war, especially, we must remember this if we want to help those who are ashamed that they suffer so and who can confide in no one.

ON THE GOOD USES OF WAR, OUR SCOURGE

Christians who freely abandon everything they possess in order to follow the Lord are, we might say, in the minority. Most Christians renounce only what has already been wrenched from their hands: they offer the sacrifice of their life only when death comes to sit on their doorstep.

God gives us many masters, but of them all war is surely the harshest. War strips man of the essential as well as the accessory; it robs him of his son and of his horse. The refugee who beds down in the haystack owns nothing but what he wears on his back. From the soldier even what he has on his back is demanded, and even he becomes an automaton who drops down to sleep and staggers up to kneel and fire, to kill and to be killed—all on order.

I know that there are certain sovereign spirits who find a kind of exultation in this orgy of spoliation. "Since I have pants and a shirt and something or other to eat," a friend writes to me, "I find myself entirely free to go forth to find Christ in my brother. On the very first day I felt this way, and on many others since then. In the mornings, I go to a little convent nearby where the Mass means more to me than ever. . . ." This man has no difficulty in believing that God has loved us and that He loves us even more tenderly today as He grinds us to dust.

But less generous spirits, those vulnerable to the temptation of despair, must concentrate hard on this one article of our faith: we are loved. What lesson could guide their meditations more truly than the prayer of Pascal "for the good usage of sickness"?

Not one word of this prayer need be changed for us to use it today, for war is an illness of the social body, each cell of which—that is to say, each family, each individual—is under attack. But the soul is miraculously preserved in the individual, free because it is separate even while it is also in thrall, for it draws its consolation from the very excess of its own travail. "How Thy scourge comforts me!" said Pascal to the Lord: this was, in fact, his prayer as he lay dying.

4. On Nature

WHERE I LIVE: MALAGAR

I have written everything about Malagar that I have
ever had on my mind or in my heart. Memories beyond
counting have crystallized around it. But the idea never
occurred to me that what I wrote would someday be
subject to inspection, as it were. The heat of childhood
summers accumulated on this terrace; this silent, flowing plain was not seen directly but as it was reflected
in eyes now closed. Indeed, Malagar existed within me,
and I never thought to compare it with this vineyard
that lies 2 miles from Langon, or with this house and
these outbuildings and these few sickly trees.

This is a drawback to notoriety that I had scarcely
expected: people now want to see this Malagar where
so many of my heroes have lived and suffered. For the
first time, I am making an effort to look at it with the
eyes of a visitor and stranger. I apply myself to seeing
what remains when I strip it of all that my imagination

178

has clothed it in, when I siphon off all the blood I have poured into it. I force the crowd of ghosts, the living and the dead and the invented, that I have set loose along these paths and under these arbors, to retreat and disappear.

What will people say when they see Malagar reduced to being only what it really is? I already have a small store of comments: "Is *that* the terrace at Malagar? . . ." "Where are the arbors? . . . What? Those straggling bushes? . . ."

Yes, what is it if not Malagar? You climb a hill in the sunlight. You cross a sorry-looking rabbit warren in front of the outhouses. This earth does not love trees, nor do the men here love them. The soil is dry and hard and gives them little nourishment. Mine are a hundred years old, but they are stunted and small. As everywhere in France, many of the elms are dying. (Our highways are lined with these corpses that do not rot and whose slow destruction gives off no odor.) Often just one branch sickens. I order it to be pruned and the tree revives and its death agony is prolonged. But sometimes the most vigorous elm is struck down by apoplexy. It shrivels all at once, like the accursed fig tree.

Once past the warren, there is the expanse of sheds, comprising the stables, the cow sheds, and the wagoners' quarters. What possessed my grandfather to build this absurd businessman's chalet on top of the hill where one can see it from thirty miles around? It dominates and overwhelms my own house, and it once led a peasant to say that Malagar looked like a *"baque escornade"* —a one-horned cow.

We come to the north side of the house. No steps lead up to it. In most of my novels, I have not hesitated to build a flight of stairs: an imaginery improvement costing nothing. I settle for a bank bordered by sage. Plain façade without ornament except for the *genoise* running along the roof that embellishes all the big houses in the Midi (it is not called *genoise* in these parts, however). My grandfather gave the main body of the house a heavy slate hat. Thank Heaven, the two wings, the wine sheds, and the laundry have kept their old round tiles. Edouard Bourget said to me, "The first thing I would do would be to get rid of that slate." But I will not ruffle the shade of my grandfather who went to such trouble to disguise his house as a castle (even to the extent of flanking it with an extra tower). Get rid of the slate? I don't want my peasants to think I'm mad!

On the west side, a broad meadow slopes gently toward the low hills of Benauge, the last foothills of this lost land "between two seas," as it is called—a countryside that I would love, I believe, even if my grandmother and my mother had not cherished it so, even if it had not enchanted André Lafon, and even if my friend had not dreamed of it as he shivered in an army tent in the Souges camp, in 1915. "The hay is perhaps already stacked in the fields, and these evenings the moon must keep watch over the sleeping roads," he wrote, in one of the last letters I received from him.

To the left, the vineyard reaches toward the west, napping in the afternoon sun or awaiting the approach of evening. These vines that to me are quick with life, now flourishing, now ailing, clasp their grapes close. They are threatened in a thousand ways—by the storms, the hail, the dog days, the rain, not to count sicknesses as numerous as those that assail human creatures. How can their master look at them with the indifferent eye of a visitor?

Now let us cross the vestibule where, like all the children of all the long vacations past, mine are sprawled on the couch, waiting for the midday heat to subside. To the south, the courtyard, with its long, low chairs, is a furnace. Two pillars intersect the panorama that is the glory of Malagar. Old arbors descend toward the terrace and the points of view—Saint-Macaire, Langon, the *landes,* Sauternes. How many times I have described this plain "on which summer presses her delirium"! The light sparkling on the tiles and vines, the silence of stupor—does all this exist "in itself"? Because it has been contemplated by people I have loved and those I have invented, this countryside has become human for me, too human, even divine. I see through it to the bones of my own people that it covers, and into each of these simple churches whose steeples mark the invisible current, the little living Host!

I will dare to say what I think: to me, this is the most beautiful country in the world, throbbing, fra-

ternal, sole in knowing what I know; sole in remember-
ing now destroyed faces of which I no longer speak to
anyone. Its evening breeze is the living, warm breath
of one of God's creatures (as if my mother embraced
me). An earth that breathes!

To the right, some arbors . . . a few clumps of trees
. . . ancient boxwood and laurels separate them from
the sun-drenched vines. To the left, an orchard . . . a
row of lindens that lengthens the vista. . . . Let us go
back to the house.

Opening off the vestibule, a large room, which I
have set aside for myself, where the flies hum in air
fresh with the smell of whitewashed walls. I have often
described *(Le Nœud de Vipères)* this mahogany, this
rosewood, these bibelots left by generations—shells carried up by successive tides. . . . A stimulating place to
work in, a veritable hothouse for a novelist, where
books come to their full growth in three weeks, where
I am driven by my demon to write so fast that I can
not decipher the afternoon's work if I do not dictate
it the same evening. A room where, when school takes
the children back to Paris, I will live alone through the
long rainy autumn evenings that smell of the wine press,
the new wine, and the mist.

This is Malagar. These few pages testify how incapable I am of giving an objective description of it. For
that matter, have I ever been able to write anything
with eyes open? I can only hope that the unknown
friends who will some day climb this hill will have no
trouble finding the old home. And since their imagina-

tion is powerful enough to let them take pleasure in my poor inventions, they will also be able to disbelieve the evidence before their eyes; they will know how to substitute for an all too real scene of country life the dark enchantment of the world where my heroes love, suffer, and die alone. Malagar could no more appear as what it is to my readers than it can to me. They will see here what others do not see. Even after my death, so long as there is a friend of my books on this earth, Malagar will pulsate with a muffled life.

But eventually this admirer, too, will fall asleep. Then Malagar will once more become a property of twenty hectares, planted with vineyards in full yield, situated in the commune of Saint-Maixant, twenty-five miles from Bordeaux, producing a good wine of the Sauterne type although it cannot claim the name. A magnificent view over the valley of the Garonne, a solid "big house," capacious outbuildings. How often I have imagined, in a survey of the area, the little pink sign "For Sale" and some newly rich horse-trader peering at the upset price.

HAIL

Newman believed that earth and sky give us an impression of purity and innocence because the natural world was created before sinful man and did not share in Adam's crime. Nevertheless because man has lived by the earth, throwing himself upon it to sleep or to weep until it engulfs him and he returns to dust, Nature has become human: she is fashioned of the ashes of human sin and in no way resembles the thing she was when she was born of the thought of God. Her appearance alone immediately betrays human needs; these fields of wheat, these vineyards are our hunger and our thirst—more than our thirst they bespeak our incurable desire for intoxication, sleep, and oblivion. And in yet another aspect, it is to be found flowering before the most modest home—the stalk of geranium, the verbena, the mignonette along the wall.

We cannot imagine the world as it was before man appeared—or at least I cannot, because I am not a traveler and have never visited any primitive places. But I doubt that uninhabited islands or virgin lands sing the glory of God as clearly as our old countries proclaim the toil and travail of man.

Perhaps I dislike traveling to faraway places because I have a horror of inhuman lands. I want the world of man to be involved in my adventure; I want it to be an inseparable part of all that I love and remember and mourn. What do I care for a landscape that has never been reflected in eyes I love? For me the horizon must preserve the imprint of a caress from glances long since dimmed. The only country I can bear to live in has long been my confidante, my accomplice. It has faithfully assumed the face that my joy or sorrow has demanded. It has modeled itself after my own heart until shaped to its very form. I remember the ardor, the clear, bright fire of these fields in the tawny days of

August when my youth was consumed by pain and desire. And it was here that my inner solitude took shape, suddenly, before my very eyes, here in the midst of this mute countryside from which no voice sounded and where roads from which Sister Anne herself could have seen no dust rise lay empty and sleeping.

Nature has become so imbued with our humanity that her ordeals become our ordeals: they are physically ours. During the terrible week in September when so many storms lashed the countryside on the eve of the grape harvest, it was not only the wine-grower in me who suffered; the hail pelted me, it attacked and wounded my body. As Mme. de Sévigné wrote to her ailing daughter, "Your chest hurts me." I suffered like that with the slashed vines and the grapes ripped bleeding from the stock. If I had been alone, I might have lifted my arms, and they would have moved in rhythm wth storm-torn branches.

But Jean-Louis Vaudoyer and Pierre Brisson were here; for the latter, a drama critic, the season was opening earlier than he had expected with a curiously plotted show complete with full orchestra. The lighting effects won special praise from them: acid green against a turbulent gray sky. Both friends sympathized with my unhappiness, surely, but how could they help admiring such a magnificent hurricane? And perhaps they were also thinking that Oscar Wilde's paradox was being verified before their eyes: Nature imitates Art. That is why the horizon familiar to the novelist who specializes

in portraying stormy hearts and climates fits harmoni-
ously into the fictional romance it has inspired and
strives to conform to it—and let the wine-grower stand
the expense!

The storm passed, and in the stunned silence, amid
a dripping of leaves like a soft rain of tears, we leaned
over the battered vineyard as if it were a martyred
child. It was not quite dead, but the wild beasts that
were still growling beyond the distant hills had mauled
it cruelly, and it was bleeding from a thousand wounds.
It makes me think of little Sainte Exupérance, whose
wax image in the somber basilica of Verdelais very
near my house has often set me dreaming. She is one
of the saints about whom we know only what is recorded in an epitaph in the catacombs—that she was a
child, a virgin, a martyr. She is resting her head on a
silken cushion, and her little girl's curls are spread
over it. On her softly swelling, dovelike throat is a tiny
wound; a trickle of bright blood is flowing from it.
And her dress of velvet and gold thread belongs to the
princess in Perrault's fairy tale who met a wolf.

The suffering vineyard lay on its hillside in the same
way. Children picked up dead birds from the road. A
neighboring wine-grower was bemoaning her losses, and
her overseer, hit even harder than she, was consoling
her: "One must take the bad weather with the good,
patronne!" The wisdom of the peasant! Take the bad
with the good. His Eminence had ordered public

prayers for rain. As far as I am concerned, I would have done well to make a pact with the drought. It is true that the soil on our property holds moisture, so that the vines can do without rain for months; they stay vigorous in the fiery furnace and throughout the torrid summers sing the canticle of the young Hebrews. But even if the vineyard must suffer for lack of water, one should never ask for rain on the eve of the grape harvest, especially when there has been none since June, for it would be a miracle if it were to come then except as a storm "bearing hail"—and who among us deserves a miracle?

The trouble is that these storms never come singly. From the thickets of the heavens, the rumbling beasts spring forth in packs, like wolves; they attack in hordes from all directions. You may hope to escape the one rearing up in the east, but the beetling monster ambushed to the south, behind the hornbeam hedges, will not fail you. Now and again he hesitates, he seems to move off, and for an hour you watch him slip northward. That is how it was, September 8 last, and we were drawing a deep breath of relief when suddenly he changed his mind; a savage icy wind hurled him down upon us. Through all the tumult we thought we could hear the trees crying out in fear.

The next day, it all began again. By two o'clock, the enemy was already on hand. From early afternoon until evening we waited for his attack, living out a kind of death agony. In the *landes,* surrounded by pines, you do not see the storms building up; there they show themselves only when they attack. But here we are spared none of the anguish of waiting. The enemy is in no hurry; he knows that his prey cannot escape, that it is bound by deep roots to the earth; and we, who could as well have been in Salzburg or Bayreuth or Juan-les-Pins, waited, chained to our vines and to a harvest dedicated to destruction.

The evening before, the vines had endured the dreadful ordeal without human help, for it was the feast of Our Lady of September, and anyone who was not drinking in the inns was praying to the Black Virgin of Verdelais. But on the 9th, the wine-growers were out hurling useless bombs and rockets at the sky, while the bell in the watchtower of Saint-Maixant—which, they say, drives the hail away—pealed loud and clear, the way a child sings at night to drive off thieves. None the less, a zeppelin of clouds, black and swollen with hail, came slipping low through the sky, peppered us lightly, spared Sauternes—where the promise of a great year was ripening, still intact—and burst finally over the *landes,* where the stoic pines are indifferent to such a pelting and, friends to somber and stormy skies, fear no scourge but the lightning.

WINTER'S LESSON

One week more, then back to Paris. It will be the end of long days gorged with reading and of endless reveries amid the pungent bonfires of vine stalks. It

will be the end of the fog that floated above the meadows for the moon to play upon, of the mists that in
the afternoons were suddenly pierced by the shafts of
the winter sun that Baudelaire speaks of. Sometimes I
would see an unknown army descend the slope, flowing, immense, along a broad front; and suddenly the
cricket would be chirping on the hearth. Then the
roads would turn black and gleaming again. A stone's
throw away (I could almost have touched it) the rain-
bow is born between two poplars. The vines—those not
yet pruned—tinge the hillsides with an indescribable
rose.

Winter in the country among the fields does not have
any of the cloistered or even shrouded feeling I had
imagined. The countryside in no way reminds one of
animals that hibernate until the spring. Everything
stays awake. The shell of the buds betrays a sap in
gestation. The comradeship of hunger unites the birds
who give no thought to love. Every morning, a pipit
flutters against my bedroom window and pecks at it
furiously. I see her soft yellow breast from close at
hand. She is not trying to get in, because the open window does not attract her. Is she, like the lark, tempted
by the mirror, obsessed by the mystery of the trans-
parent?

These are the things that occupy my mind while all
that I hold most dear is in its death throes. And yet the
destiny of the world is rolling on, and crevasses yawn
everywhere; the signs of Europe's inner travail and dis-
location.

Despite this anguish? No, because of the anguish. Montaigne, Shakespeare, Retz, Rivarol, and Stendhal wrote and meditated and dreamed in periods as somber as this; they sustained the spiritual life of France, of all Europe, that survives the horrors of party strife and war; they fed the human tide that no political outrage or crime can stem, and there is no presumption or vanity in including oneself among them: the least among us who has been granted the vocation of writer counts for one moment of this continuity.

The nobility of every thinking person lies in the power of mastering himself through reflection. These hills sleeping under the fog, their silence broken only by the clopping of a schoolboy's shoes as he walks along some lost road; these cloudy afternoons of reading the old masters, now returned to dust, whose books reveal secrets the authors did not dare share with their living friends—these things attract one who is habitually inclined to the study of man and of self, and invite him to redouble his attention. The peasants around me redouble their efforts, too, and throw themselves into their work with a will; the men keep at their pruning until the light has gone and the clicking of their shears makes me dream of insects that would sing in wintertime.

All things continue. There is no such thing in history as catastrophe, at least in the dictionary sense of a final event. Were astonishment an attribute of God, He would surely be amazed to see that war still disconcerts men. What powerful nation was ever exempt from the repeated tests of strength that we are being forced to endure? No empire is know to have existed since the world began whose masters have not had to prove daily and hourly that they were powerful enough to face every attack without giving an inch.

But nothing is happening today so untoward that we are forbidden to keep a free and inquiring mind. We have no more right than Montaigne to interrupt our long rumination of ideas and speculations and dreams. . . .

The light is fading. The last tatter of leaves flutters on the old elms. The nudity of winter is already tinged with the color of spring. If I were to fall into a sleep lasting several months and rouse to find myself in this same countryside, I would think I were awaking in a March twilight, for as the year declines Nature seems to be returning to her infancy.

François Mauriac was born at Bordeaux, France, in 1885 and educated in that city at Roman Catholic schools and at Bordeaux University. "The history of Bordeaux," he says, "is the history of my body and my soul: it is my childhood and my youth crystallized."

Mauriac undertook philosophical studies at the Ecole des Chartes in Paris, but gradually abandoned scholarship for the writing of fiction. *A Kiss for the Leper,* a novel written in 1922, quickly made him famous; and his writings since that time have won him world renown. In 1933 he was elected a member of the French Academy. Shortly afterward he began his controversial writings which he continued during the years of resistance under the name of Forez, and in 1945 became a brilliant leader-writer on *Le Figaro.* In 1952 M. Mauriac won the Nobel Prize: a fitting recognition of the original type of novel he has evolved and of his many admirable plays. In 1959, Mauriac was elected an honorary member of the American Academy of Arts and Letters. Of *The Son of Man,* a meditation on Christ's life which The World Publishing Company issued in 1960, *The Atlantic Monthly* said that "the author's emotion and the dense eloquence of his style ultimately produce an effect close to that of poetry."